Promise & Potential

A Life of
Wisdom
Courage
Strength
and Will

Scott F. Paradis

Promise & Potential
A Life of Wisdom, Courage, Strength and Will

Book and cover design by 1106 Design, Phoenix, Arizona

Published and distributed by:

CORNERSTONE ACHIEVEMENTS

Cornerstone Achievements
Post Office Box 256
Mount Vernon, Virginia 22121

www.cornerstone-achievements.com

ISBN-13: 978-0-9798638-1-3 (Hardcover)
ISBN-10: 0-9798638-1-3 (Hardcover)

Library of Congress Control Number (LCCN): 2007905931

1st Printing January 2008

Printed in the United States of America

Promise & Potential

This is my prayer for you.

May God Grant You:

Wisdom to find your way,

Courage to proceed,

Strength to overcome,

And Will to persevere.

Recognize the promise,

Fulfill the potential!

Ignorant people are unable, even unto death, to abandon the idea that in the fingertip of words there is the meaning itself, and will not grasp ultimate reality because of their intent to cling to words.

- Lankavatara Sutra -

Words exist because of meaning; once you've gotten the meaning, you can forget the words.

- Chuang Tzu -

Preface

Language, particularly written language, for all its beauty, subtlety, and strength, fails the task of complete expression. Insightful ideas captured and reduced to words, however, still serve as useful tools to help us crawl, inch by inch, toward our inevitable destination. Sometimes on rare, extraordinary occasions language strikes a chord of spirit and resonates a heretofore unfathomable truth in a simple, heartfelt way allowing us to bound forward and transform our experience of life. *Promise and Potential* is intended as a simple, meaningful, inspirational, and enjoyable expression of at least some part of truth.

To follow convention, the first time a writer or speaker quotes someone, he or she may be obliged to identify that person by name, "As Mr. Smith once said..." The next time that communicator draws on a familiar quote he or she might rather say, "As it has been said…" But, the third time the speaker or writer quotes another, he or she can safely exclaim, "As I always say…" Consider this writing our third passage. I claim no credit for an original idea and apologize up front for not lending credibility to a statement or expression which I fail to attribute to someone famous. The words and ideas expressed here through this medium ought to stand alone.

The philosopher Blaise Pascal once expressed a sentiment later echoed by Henry David Thoreau: "Excuse the length of my writing for it would require more time to be brief." Here I have attempted to assemble the essence of the ideas and concepts to bring your ultimate destiny into focus. You may find the brevity on some subjects, concepts, or ideas somewhat frustrating. If the presentation leaves you wanting more please consult the resources listed in the acknowledgments.

Contents

Foreword

"Preach the Gospel at all times, but use words only if absolutely necessary." This directive subtly identifies the paradox of human life, the dichotomy between words and actions, the difference between life through our minds and thoughts and life experienced through our feelings and emotions in an environment of time and space. Examining the distinction reveals who we are.

Promise & Potential attempts first to define, in the limited form of written language, what life is about. Second, *Promise & Potential* is a humble attempt to enlighten and inspire.

My prayer is that these words, appealing to both intellect and emotion, expose that divine spark within. And that with just a little focus and care that spark ignites a bonfire of enthusiasm, joy, and peace to become a beacon for a pale and frightened world.

As ideas are neither unique nor personal — that is, owned or created by an individual — the ideas presented in *Promise & Potential* are not new, revolutionary, or groundbreaking. True wisdom is simple and timeless. These ideas contain a truth expressed and experienced by sages and saints, simple and blessed people. *Promise & Potential* is an attempt to help you connect more deeply with ultimate truth; see with new vision; hear with new clarity; and act with new purpose to fulfill the promise and potential that is you.

Each life is a note in the grand symphony of God, each person's story a chapter in the magnificent epic. These pages of metaphors, analogies, and parables attempt to reveal and enlighten a glimmer of the truth within.

My prayer for you is that you will accept on faith that your life is one of promise and potential. God intends for you, to have life and have it more abundantly. I pray that through your faith you recognize the wisdom of your next step; muster the courage to take that step; realize the strength to face your fears; and focus your will to joyfully persevere. Your time to act is short, but the bliss of an enduring moment, enveloped in the embrace of love, will last for eternity.

It has been said, "Life is what happens while we prepare for the future or recover from the past." Life is that wonderful slice of experience that if we are not paying attention, we may miss altogether. It is time we find the peace, joy, and love of the enduring moment.

May you find your center and in so doing inspire others to recognize the promise and fulfill the potential.

Promise and Potential

. . . that you might have life and have it more abundantly.

- John 10:10 -

Something More...

Imagine a place not too far from where you are today, in a time not unlike our own. A remote village stood in a deep valley isolated from the outside world. The valley, once a happy, prosperous place, over time had lost its warmth and light — the people there had lost their way. Simple challenges matured into difficult problems. Over time the village inhabitants came to expect and endure repeated maladies. Plagued by drought, famine, storms, and earthquakes, the villagers lost hope — dreams failed and happiness faded to distant memory.

Joy and laughter, which once bubbled in harmony with crisp mountain streams, dried with the parched earth and plunged into the dark shadows of the mountains. Life grew more ominous with each passing season. Eventually the air itself became stagnant and listless, heavy with anguish. The valley, once the bosom of life, was now a desolate and desperate place.

The people who inhabited the valley, once cooperative, now competed aggressively for dwindling resources. In the space of a generation, the fading memory of better times transformed into the speculation of legend. The legend was of an age of prosperity, a time when fruit was plentiful, and water flowed deep and clear — an age long dead and buried.

The villagers scratched out a meager hand-to-mouth existence. They learned to guard any excess in anticipation for shortages sure to follow. The mood of these people was best described as one of despair. The people lost hope in what was, and lacked a vision for what might be.

One day, one ordinary day, a stranger appeared strolling casually along a path toward the village. The stranger, dressed in a fashion similar to the villagers, carried in each hand a ripe red apple. He casually acknowledged each stupefied passerby and observer with a friendly greeting. He sauntered confidently into the village, munching one of those crisp, juicy apples. The village people were amazed and bewildered by the appearance of this stranger. They wondered first, where did he come from? Any passes into or out of the valley had long been blocked. And, with even greater intrigue, they wondered, where did he get the fruit he feasted upon? Only the oldest of the villagers could recall a harvest producing fruit as exquisite as this man possessed.

Emboldened by the stranger's disarming manner some villagers approached the man. He readily exchanged greetings with them and patiently answered their questions. He had come down from the hills after having passed through the mountains. The fruit he bore was from orchards on the far side of the mountains. At the villagers' urging he proclaimed the bounty of the land from where he had come. The sun was bright, rain was plentiful, water was clear and fresh. On the vast plains and rolling hills stretching from the mountains to the sea the people had plenty of food and readily shared the treasure of the land's bounty.

Astonished by the stranger's descriptions of the world beyond the imprisoning mountains, the walls that loomed over the dismal valley, the villagers brought the stranger before their elders. Though the tale was attractive, hard times had made the people rigid and skeptical. The wise and suspicious elders would interrogate the stranger and discern the truth, exposing any lie.

The elders, upon seeing the stranger themselves and hearing his tales, feared this man could only usher in more calamities the townspeople could ill afford to endure. The stranger patiently and in as much detail as his interrogators demanded answered every question posed to him. After a short consultation and not unexpectedly, the elders declared the stranger a charlatan. No one could pass through the mountains nor scale its peaks. Many had, in desperation tried, and many had failed. The valley was cut off from the outside world; its inhabitants were destined for ruin.

The stranger explained how he had come to enter the valley through a tunnel in the side of one mountain. The elders forcefully rebuked his claim. Those tunnels were once mines long since abandoned. They believed none of those shafts passed through the mountains. The stranger, bemused and saddened by the hardened hearts he faced, nevertheless offered to prove his claim. "I shall leave this apple with you to savor and share; tomorrow I will return with a basket of fruit from the vineyards and orchards on the far side of the mountains." Amazed at this offer, but still doubting his claims, the elders dismissed the stranger. The stranger for his part graciously excused himself and wandered into the hills.

Word spread throughout every household in the village. Never in memory had such anticipation been kindled. The villagers debated late into the night the veracity of the stranger's claims. Though the people were utterly amazed at what they had seen, most remained convinced that no one could navigate the mountains. This stranger, though he had made his way once, would never be seen nor heard from again.

Dawn broke the next day like most did in the valley, a hazy pale light. The villagers went about their chores but each kept a keen eye turned toward the hills and an alert ear tuned for any hint of the stranger. As the sun peaked in the sky the stranger emerged from the shadowy forest. As he had promised he carried a basket of ripe fruit to share with the villagers.

The villagers with some glee and trepidation hurriedly assembled in the town square. Smiles and smirks surrounded the stranger. His return was both jubilant and vexing. The elders imposed a calm upon the crowd. Then these self-proclaimed stewards and protectors began an inquisition with the purpose to prove what they themselves already knew. There was nothing else for these villagers, no opportunity outside this valley, nothing but a slow death on the horizon. This stranger was a fraud and a hoax.

The elders began again. How did the stranger get here? By what means did he pass through the impenetrable mountains? Where did the fruit come from? How could this be?

As he had the previous day, the stranger calmly and politely responded to every question and addressed every doubt. The villager's spirits stirred with each word. The people marveled at the stranger's description of the world beyond the valley and his account of the route to travel there. Even if the tale he crafted was a lie the people felt they could ease the burden of their daily grind by stepping outside their reality and embracing a hope that something far better might exist. The elders, for their part, sensed a willingness among the people to accept these wild claims. This only intensified their resolve to reveal the deception and prove the stranger a fake.

The stranger spoke of a vast and fertile land beyond the mountains with clean, fresh water and fields of dark rich soil yielding a plentiful harvest. The people inhabiting these distant lands were peaceful and filled with joy. They counted their blessings and shared readily with any in need. The stranger, understanding the state of despair that had for so long dominated these people, offered to show the way.

The elders balked at the offer. Even if those abandoned mine shafts could lead through the mountains the route must be treacherous, the way fraught with peril. Who could guarantee their safety? And, furthermore, if they did succeed in reaching the other side, who was to know whether what the stranger said was true? Could some forces of evil be waiting to enslave the villagers? Or worse?

The stranger gazed kindly around the gathered throng. He saw faces worn and drawn from endless toil and ravaged by lack of hope. He observed backs slumped and spirits long broken. Even the young among them lacked the enthusiasm of youth. This forbidding valley had drained the very lifeblood of possibility, the prospect of joy. The stranger moved with compassion, turned to the crowd to offer an alternative to this meager existence.

"Choose a handful among you to accompany me into the tunnel and pass through the mountain. I will show these select few, the bountiful harvest and introduce them to the friendly people waiting on the other side. Your kinfolk can, then, bring the message of truth, prosperity, and promise, back to your village. They, in turn, can make clear the way for all those who desire to follow."

With these words, the offer was extended to the people. Who among them would brave the passage? Who among them would accept the challenge, take the risk? The villagers remained silent and still. The spark of hope the stranger had kindled through his words of abundance and prosperity faded like the last ember in a cold fire pit before the resistance of hardened hearts. The elders remained resolute in their rejection of any opportunity outside this valley and steadfast in their claims of disaster for any villager who would tempt fate and join this stranger. The fear was palpable, the danger real. As painful an existence as life in the valley was, the danger beyond knowing was more frightful, more ominous, more real.

Finally, one young woman broke the silence and cried out, "I will go with you." Every villager turned in disbelief. It seemed that someone would risk life itself on only a stranger's word and a basket of fruit as evidence. The young woman's father spoke up: "You cannot go, I forbid it." The woman turned to her father and replied, "I must go." She continued, "Father, I love you dearly, but never in my life have we been offered an opportunity to escape this dying valley and begin anew. We struggle more and more, every day, for less and less. The path we are on is surely toward our destruction." The father looked upon his daughter's hopeful face and said, "You could be killed." Tears of regret streamed from her eyes, and she responded, "Then if I die, I will die awash in hope."

The father immediately grasped the futility of trying to dissuade his daughter. Her newly kindled strength fanned his own ember of hope. "Then I will go with you," he said. The victory the young women had won over her fear, fueled growing hope and courage. Others stepped forward. In the relative safety of the village square, though anxious and with little confidence of the result, a dozen or more joined the stranger.

"What shall we bring? How shall we prepare? When shall we go?" was the clamor of questions coming from the unlikely volunteers. The stranger reassured the group, "The way is not difficult. Let us go as we are. We are ready now." And with that they set off.

The elders scorned the group as the stranger led them off: "Your family and friends will mourn your loss as their trials only multiply by your abandoning them."

Many of the villagers followed the party up into the hills. Maybe there was a chance that the stranger spoke the truth. As the stranger led the group higher into the mountains, the weaker ones fell off the trail and returned home. Soon a storm began to blow. Most of the onlookers headed for shelter. The stranger seemed undeterred in the face of the storm. He reassured the group of volunteers they would find relief in the shelter of the tunnel.

After a few hours of hiking the group's enthusiasm began to wane. One by one the remaining onlookers dropped off and faded away. Though the stranger noticed their passing he drew no attention to those who chose another path. Upon finally seeing the entrance to the old abandoned mineshaft, the resolve of some volunteers fell victim to fear. Though they had not yet ventured beyond their known world, the words of the elders echoed in their heads and bred fear in their hearts. They abandoned the quest before it had begun in earnest. Only five steadfast souls, led by the young women and her father, dared venture into the mineshaft with the stranger.

The cavern was cold and dark, the blackness desiring to extract the very breath of life. The still air was dank and heavy, the way foreboding. As the stranger lit a torch in the cramped tunnel, the darkness withdrew. Beyond the torchlight, however, the darkness appeared eager to consume any unfortunate life that stumbled into its abyss. The scaly walls creaked and the molten earth trembled. Pain-filled moans rumbled forth from the deep. Two more villagers, overwhelmed by the prospect before them, abandoned the stranger. They retreated for the relative safety of the storm. The stranger, undaunted, beckoned the remaining voyagers forward. He explained, "I will show you the way. All you must do is trust me. Step where I tell you to step. Leap when I tell you to leap. The journey is not long. Just ignore what you see and hear and step with a light step. Your reward awaits."

Driving rain, howling wind, flashing lightning, and grumbling thunder were at the voyagers' heels. Ahead lay a passage, dark, cramped, and ominous — beckoning as if to Hell itself. One single beacon, borne by a humble, self-assured man was to light the way. As the stranger advanced and the walls closed in, for all but one sojourner the last flicker of hope faded. The decision point was breached — all faith must go to the stranger or the traveler must strike a hasty retreat — life itself hung in the balance. The young woman's father and one other remaining traveler finally succumbed to fear. The two retreated to the entrance of the tunnel. Demons, nurtured in the minds of the weary, carried the day. A life of little hope and even less promise seemed more inviting than facing the fears of this deep. The daughter called out, "Don't worry, father, I will return."

One faithful, trusting, brave young woman journeyed on. She listened to the stranger's comforting voice. She stepped when he asked her to step. She leapt when he asked her to leap. She trod lightly placing her feet upon the footing he provided. She listened not to the sounds emanating from the walls but rather to a calm, quiet, comforting voice. She gave no quarter to the thoughts attempting to sway her from her goal; to the fear battling to rise to her consciousness. She refused to shackle herself to fear but rather in acceptance and peace she fixed her gaze, secured her trust, and basked in the light. She ventured forth, she carried on.

In a short time the stranger put up the torch, fixing it to a holder on the wall. He congratulated the young woman for making the journey as together they emerged from the tunnel. They were bathed in brilliant sunshine, unlike anything the woman had experienced in the shadowy valley. The beauty of the sight they beheld was beyond description. Joy and sadness welled up together within the young women as she fell to her knees in tears. "To think," she muttered, "I have been only a short distance from this bounty all my life. My neighbors, my friends, my family have all struggled in misery, ransoming their very lives to toil in our dying valley because we were afraid to even envision an alternative." The stranger lovingly acknowledged both her joy and her grief.

The pair sat for some time overlooking a vast plain and rolling green hills. The young woman reflected on what this meant for herself, her family, and all the villagers of the lost valley. After some time had passed, the stranger spoke: "You now know the way. It is up to you to show others the way through their fears to a better life."

The journey of faith revealed a new and glorious mission for this young soul. Her task in life became to show the way, make easy the path. Joy and prosperity wait for those who dismiss fear and instead embrace the promise and potential of life.[1]

Guy Finley, an author and teacher of spiritual principles from southern Oregon, used this story of an isolated village in one of his talks to illustrate a point about fear and faith — the struggle of human frailty.

Does the theme of this story strike a chord with you? Have you heard the story before, perhaps told in a different way? Does this tale sound similar to the story told of a man from Galilee who walked dusty roads some two thousand years ago? Have circumstances changed in the intervening two millennia? Has humanity evolved at all?

Reality is merely an illusion,
albeit a very persistent one.

- Albert Einstein -

Something More Than Physical Reality Exists

Is This All There Is?

The ultimate question of a searcher is, "**Is this it?**" Is the world we experience through our senses, the dimensions of time, space, and matter; the environment, and the life forms inhabiting the environment; the circumstances, the direction, and the outcomes of life: is this it?

Is this all there is? Is life a fleeting and repeating series of what we've seen, where we've been, and what we've done?

We pause and ponder, on occasion: Does life have a purpose? Does my life have a purpose? Where do I go from here? Where can I go from here?

The searcher, by definition, is not content with what is. The searcher is looking for that something more, the light in the darkness, hope in despair, calm in the storm, or one missing piece to make the puzzle whole and complete.

As you read these words you sense that something more exists — something more real, something more true, some greater whole. Only once we accept the truth that "there is something more" can we move beyond isolation and embrace a new, fuller life.

What we want, hope for, dream about, seek, is to have life and have it more abundantly. We can know no greater gift than to have life abundantly. When we accept the promise of our lives and embrace the potential of our existence in this time, place, and circumstance we release our chains and usher in new found freedom to create and experience ultimate peace and joy.

– Love truly, radically, springs eternal. –

We have not power to make the sun rise,
Or to keep stars from twinkling.
We can't control the seasons or the tides.
We can't make a flower grow,
Or change another's mind.
We can, however, play a part in all these things.
Though we are not the whole,
We contribute to the whole,
And by our being,
Make the whole complete.

Usually we accept, without question, the physical reality around us, the boundaries defined by earth, sea, and sky. Similarly we accept the body is real, as are the things we sense in the environment. We accept the things surrounding us as a matter of course, without reservation, and often without consideration.

You are sitting on something. You have a ceiling (or sky) above you and a floor (or earth) below. Air surrounds you. We accept these things, our surroundings, the objects in our environment, as real. But, what does real mean? How do we know?

Of course we can verify physical phenomena. We confirm the substance of this reality, the rules these substances conform to, through our senses. We consult with one another, collaborate on what we experience through our senses — sight, hearing, touch, taste, smell — to ultimately agree on what "is." This is the same wherever we travel on this planet. We agree, so it must be so — or is it?

Consider, for a moment, very carefully, very profoundly, that the physical reality we know and experience is not all there is.

When the wind blows, though we see branches sway and hear leaves rustle, do we see the wind? We don't see the wind, only its effects. Does that mean the wind is not real?

When man believed the world was flat — was it? No. The belief the world was flat limited opportunities. People dared not venture out to sea. Like the villagers in our opening story, fear and clinging to the known served only to constrain life.

If someone, sometime, did not envision a possibility that others could not see, if someone did not first consider the idea of "something more," we would still be living a subsistence existence. Man could not fly, space travel would still be fantasy; as would the generation, distribution, and application of electricity;

Unless you believe
you will not understand.

- Isaiah 7:9 -

the internal combustion engine; the telephone; the television; the computer. All technological advances, and even the complexity of human society, began as ideas — ideas most people held as unachievable, unrealistic, undesirable — beyond belief.

In practical terms, the idea of "something beyond our senses exists" is not difficult to accept. Mankind has discovered and exploited ranges of energy beyond the reach of our physical senses. We can communicate around the globe, we can look through objects using light, sound, and magnetic forces, and we can power machinery using forces our biology cannot detect. These are but a glimpse of endless possibilities yet to unfold, yet to explore.

Skeptics, as skeptics through the ages have asserted, claim man has reached the limit of his advance. Skeptics cling to an understanding of what is through what they acknowledge and experience. By clinging to this idea of "what is must and can only be defined through our senses," skeptics rationalize and limit the possibilities of life. Skeptics proclaim, as they have through the ages, "The intellect is king, long live the king."

I sense you, at your core, are not a skeptic. To even explore the idea that something beyond your understanding exists is outside the capacity of a true skeptic. Like the villagers in our lost valley, skeptics would rather remain in the darkness of the known than awaken to the light.

Something beyond this reality in space, bounded by time, exists. We can unlock aspects of that hidden something in a very personal way. Beyond our physical senses are areas few of us explore or develop: intuition, psychic abilities, and undefined phenomena. Skeptics deny the existence of these phenomena and powers as vehemently as some asserted the earth was flat, flight was impossible, and wireless communication a fantasy. But the truth is, life has promise and potential

Blessed are they,
who have not seen,
yet still believe.

- John 20:29 -

beyond a skeptic's imagining. We must embrace the risk to have life abundantly.

Throughout history, by some means, the impossible became possible. Through a combination of ideas and action, what could be became what was. Opportunity existed for something more, then, in the same way that opportunity still exists today. Something beyond what we "know" and what we experience in this physical reality exists. Each and every one of us has the potential for so much more.

For better or for worse what you experience is not all there is. "This" is not "it." We are dancing in a dream, on the edge of a vast and glorious reality waiting to be embraced, explored and experienced. What we know is only shadows on the wall relative to the vast expanse of the unknown. The key is to recognize what we do not see is not unknowable.

We grow when we accept and believe there is something to grow into. Our individual journey, in our own way and time, is through a rich and bountiful universe. Experience reveals but a fraction of the endless possibilities that await. We must begin the journey on faith, face our fears, and navigate the tunnel to reach the bountiful harvest.

"This" is not all there is.

Within this world, within the confines of personal experience, we have options. We can choose to experience reality in a positive or negative way or over a wide range in between. We can expect and accept, for better or for worse. We have a multitude of realities available to us here and now. And beyond this reality are other worlds, other dimensions, other adventures. This life is a life of promise and potential.

I stand in awe
Of surf and sea
Of moon and stars
And wind and trees
The sky above
The earth beneath
Belie grandeur
Beauty
Power
Far, far greater
Than me.

Something Organizes and Animates Experience

Something more powerful than me…

Observe nature's systems and cycles: harmony and symmetry are features of the natural world. Everything appears to operate in rhythmic, regular cycles. The blooming of flowers, the behavior of cats, the flow of water, the seasons brought on by the position of the sun, children at play, all follow describable patterns. We experience and are part of a mutually dependent environment, a system. Order and purpose underlie this system.

Children, and even imaginative adults, occasionally lose themselves in the fantasy of being a superhero, someone with superhuman powers. The superhero possesses the knowledge, the strength, the abilities, and therefore the confidence to do things far beyond the capabilities of ordinary mortals. In our everyday adult lives, though this fantasy remains appealing, we face a different reality. We can't, in fact, control the stars, whip up the wind, nor at times get our car to start. Often the mundane circumstances of life leave us feeling powerless and helpless — hardly a superhero.

Who or what is in charge? Apparently not me!

Great spiritual teachers across the centuries point to something more, some ultimate, true reality distinct from mundane existence, a reality beyond what we see, beyond what we can see, a reality that transcends our senses — fulfilling beyond measure.

Jesus' teaching leads us toward, shows us a way, from the bondage of the physical world to a liberated reality. The Buddha's way of enlightenment points out all life is suffering. By accepting the premise of life as suffering we can move beyond limitation. We may then be free to choose the path of ultimate reality to fulfillment. The Hindu tradition presents the mystery of birth and rebirth as a soul journey into and out of a reality beyond our senses. These traditions suggest spirits come into this world to experience for a higher purpose.

That the universe was formed by a fortuitous concourse of the atoms, I will no more believe than the accidental jumbling of the alphabet should fall into a most ingenious treatise on Philosophy.

- Jonathan Swift -

Compare one life, one part of the whole, to a finger on a hand. That finger is an important part of the body. It is a useful tool, an important receptor. It joins the body in rejoicing or shares in feeling pain and discomfort. The finger's destiny is tied to the body, but the body can go on without the finger. So too is one lifetime. The perspective a person brings to life contributes to the whole but is not the whole. Something greater than self designed, animates, and controls life.

My wife, Lisa, laughs when I routinely reduce complex circumstances to a few options. Limiting choices serves intellect. The options are cleverly (at least I think so) designed as to include every potential event or occurrence within what scheme suits my purpose. If I'm making the rules I can define the set as to include all potential outcomes. You can do that when you make the rules.

Regarding our mortal lives, in this "reality," I offer three possibilities:

1. Consciousness is a freak of nature: it is the manifestation of a unique combination of chemistry and biology in a dynamic environment without cause or meaning, a random event. A human lifetime is like the blooming of a flower, a chance occurrence in time and space, nothing more. Upon death, awareness ceases and the chemical process stops. A human life has no individual or collective purpose; it is pure biological probability.
2. Consciousness is the fleeting realization of a perspective. Awareness is the product of a purpose beyond intellect. The energy of a will animates in this reality allowing the temporary condition of individual experience. An individual identity serves no enduring purpose. Upon the body's death, life energy moves on; it has no individual identity.
3. Consciousness is awareness defined temporarily in time and space. The body is a vehicle, a tool to experience.

Something greater than self animates and organizes "reality."

> A force beyond comprehension animates reality. Every life offers a unique perspective endowed with identity existing outside the confines of time and space. Every individual life contributes to the whole. Upon the death of the body the identity assumes a new perspective.

The distinction between options two and three is the idea of the existence of an identity, an individual character with traits and purpose.

Why do we fear death so? Because in death we risk losing our identity, what we call our "self". We fear death because it is the end of what we are convinced is "me."

In truth, the grief of death is not in the pain of the body dying but rather the loosening of the ego's hold on the identity of self.

The anticipation of death, the exhilaration in dying, is in realizing the next step, a new journey, a new perspective. If we believe the death of the body is the end, we cling to what we know with all our being. We fear change because there may be no "I" in the next reality; in unity of spirit. We risk transition to a new realm of being, a heaven or a hell. For those without faith — quite a risk.

In the movie *Rudy,* a true story of a young man attempting to fulfill his dream of playing football for Notre Dame, a priest speaking with the title character explains, "In over thirty years of study I've learned two things: there is a God; and I'm not him." The mysteries of this reality escape our understanding. We claim accident, we point out chaos, but we observe consistency of order: flow, system and cycle; all evidence that something beyond our comprehension is guiding destiny.

Something greater than us controls what is. We, in separate individual forms, are subject to that power. Life is not a chance occurrence. We exist to fulfill a great and noble purpose. We exist for self and we exist for all.

The master plan
Is out of our hands.

Caught in the river,
The expanse is broad,
The banks are steep,
The current unforgiving,
The water runs deep.

Our choice,
Here now:

Go with the current,
Accept twists and turns,
Tumultuous rapids,
Peaceful water.

Or resist the flow,
And struggle,
Attempting to force the great river,
To submit to our will.

Some power greater than ourselves animates our experience, has caused us to be. What sustains us, energizes us, moves us is the thought of God. Joy is not to be found in the illusion of what surrounds us in this reality. True joy is realized by accepting the journey through this reality.

The circumstances we find ourselves in are temporary conditions — conditions we manifest, or assume to exploit, explore and experience this physical reality. The physical reality is what we say, for convenience sake, is. These temporary conditions of experience are not us.

Ultimate reality is that truth we cannot know through our senses. Ultimate reality is beyond intellect, beyond reason. Though we experience aspects of it in all we see, feel, and do, we can know it only through our higher selves. We know something beyond this time and space exists only through faith. Faith in something greater than the partial whole we see is that aspect of reality we sense deep inside. We yearn to be whole. Another reality is ultimate reality.

So, on the one hand, we have a physical reality that is easy to verify and, as it is tangible, is seemingly simple to understand. We experience physical reality through our senses every day in concrete ways. On the other hand we have ultimate reality, which is mysterious and, for most of us, seemingly difficult, if not impossible to understand, accept, acknowledge, or know.

The pinnacle of those means to experience physical reality and the truth of ultimate reality is acceptance or openness. The path from isolation, desolation, and despair to the truth of prosperity, freedom, peace, and joy is the way of faith.

The promise and potential we realize in life corresponds in great measure to the degree to which we accept and are open to life's limitless possibilities.

I look to another,
For all I have, am, can be,
My breath, senses, heartbeat,
Are all a gift to me;

My purpose,
Grand or small,
A mission to fulfill,
To laugh, to sing, to crawl,
To dance, to cry, to till;

I feel the wind,
Sense the night,
Mission?
To live each day right;

For Thy will
I'm here,
Lest I not forget,
You are always near.

Promise and Potential

✦ Something more than this physical reality exists. ✦

✦ Something organizes and animates experience. ✦

Our understanding of this life colors the reality we experience. Most of humanity binds itself into the drudgery of an isolated, perilous existence — like the lost villagers. While the often-misunderstood truth is that our boundaries are not static or fixed; home is not here, and we can go home. Something outside physical reality exists.

A power, beyond our own, organizes and animates what we experience. When we limit ourselves, we follow the script. Conflict, challenge, and effort are component parts of the drama, lending depth, texture, and context, a credibility the ego demands. But we need not revel in the drama; we have a choice, and we can choose another way.

Life is infinitely more than the limited physical reality we readily accept. Understanding that another reality exists is beyond intellect, in the realm of faith. Faith in an ultimate truth requires a willingness to move beyond intellect to be open to a truth that seeks to reveal itself to us.

Our very existence, our awareness of life and this physical reality, is like a dream. Yet buried in the dream is a gift, a promise granted us. The promise is one of opportunity and adventure, risk nestled in security. The power that animates and energizes this physical reality offers alternatives. We have unlimited resources and vast potential to draw on to discover and create in this playground. But to discover the truth we must choose to follow the guide to lead us home.

Sages and saints guide us to doorways of spirit. We can choose to be open to the promise and potential of an unlimited life of peace, love, and joy, or we can succumb to the weight of the drama. The promise is a life of unlimited potential. We need only orient on the promise and potential of each life…

…that you may have life, and have it more abundantly.

May you discover:

Wisdom to recognize your path,
Courage to navigate its course,
Strength to overcome obstacles,
And Will to joyfully endure.

Wisdom

to Accept to find your way

Know the truth and the truth will set you free.
- JOHN 8:32 -

Thou shalt have no false gods before me.
- EXODUS 20:3 -

In the Beginning...

The sky was a deep crimson blue, the air a sweet damp wrap enveloping rich fertile soil. The land blossomed with life in lush green forests and across wide sweeping plains. The oceans, lakes, rivers, and streams pulsed with life-giving energy over the face of the earth. The Creator smiled, pleased with his handiwork. He brought forth creatures of every size and shape to inhabit the vast playground he had fashioned. And as time went by He determined to bring forth a creature, not unlike himself, that could conceive of its own condition, chart a course — create its own destiny — thereby producing for the Creator his most complex and interesting experience yet.

The Creator formed a man out of the soil of the earth and breathed into him the breath of life. Man became a living being. The Creator put the man in a garden he called Eden to till it and to keep it. The man was to be one with all the creatures of the earth, living in harmony with the land and the cycle of the seasons.

The man was free, but for one restriction: of every tree of the Garden the man could freely eat; but of the tree of the knowledge of good and evil, the man should not eat; for if he did he would surely lose his way and die.

The man enjoyed his existence in paradise — warm sun, fresh water, bountiful fruit, friendly animals, and engaging work — yet somehow in the midst of this abundance he felt incomplete. The Creator, sensing the man should not be alone, made a woman and brought her to him. Though the man and woman were without clothes they were not ashamed. In the Garden there was nothing to hide from and nothing to hide.

Now the serpent was more subtle than all the wild beasts in paradise. The serpent schemed for a change. One fateful day as the woman reclined in the shade of a tree, the serpent engaged her in conversation. The serpent asked the woman, "Truly are you not to eat of any tree of the Garden?" The woman replied, "We may eat the fruit of all the trees of the Garden; but the fruit of the tree in the midst of the Garden, we shall not eat, nor touch it, lest we lose our way and die."

The serpent, incredulous at such a prospect, implored the woman, "You shall not surely die; for the day you eat of that tree, your eyes shall be opened, and you shall be like gods, knowing good and evil."

The woman carefully considered the serpent's words. This idea of being like gods and of having power beyond life in the

Garden intrigued her. She approached the tree. The tree itself was a delight to look at. The fruit it bared looked succulent and juicy — good for food, and pleasant to the touch. The woman picked some fruit, sniffed its fragrance and brought it to her lips. How could something so appealing be forbidden? She tasted the fruit. It was more wonderful than she had imagined; she ate.

Finding the fruit so pleasing the woman determined to share some with her husband. She brought some fruit to the man who recognized it was from the tree. She assured him it was wonderful, a delight to the eye and to the tongue, so he ate. Together, at once, their eyes were opened. The serpent's words to the woman bore a distasteful truth. A foreign feeling aroused in them a knowing they had not experienced before, a foreboding. That feeling forever shattered the simplicity of the bliss that had always been theirs. They felt for the first time a glimmer of doubt, the seed of fear — they knew that they were naked, and they were afraid.

Now the Creator, as he did in the cool of the day, was passing through the Garden. Realizing the Creator was near, the man and the woman hid themselves among the trees. The Creator, wishing to enjoy fellowship with the man and woman, called out to them. The Creator had sensed the change the man and woman had experienced, and He called out again. After some hesitation, the man answered the Creator saying, "I heard your voice in the Garden, but realized I was naked, so I hid myself."

The Creator, understanding immediately what had happened, asked the man, "Who told you that you were naked? Have you eaten of the tree that was forbidden?" The man replied meekly, "The woman brought me fruit from the tree, telling me it was wonderful, so I ate."

The Creator turned to the woman and asked, "What is this that you have done?" The woman replied, "The serpent tricked me, and I ate." The Creator admonished her, "You have made your choice; for your part, you will experience pain in this life, and dependence — your husband shall rule over you."

To the man the Creator said, "Because you ignored my warning, listening to the voice of another, and have eaten of the tree, in sorrow shall you eat the fruits of it all the days of your life; thorns and thistles shall it bring forth. You shall eat herbs of the field. By the sweat of your brow and the cunning of your intellect shall you eat bread, and find enmity among the creatures of the earth until you return to the ground. For out of the ground you were taken; dust you are, and to dust you shall return."[2]

The Creator had warned the man and woman not to eat from the tree at the center of the Garden. The beguiling serpent, however, pointed out that if they ate the man and woman would have the power of gods — the ability to discern right from wrong. The treasure they secured through their act of defiance was a false idol. The man and woman staked their lives on knowledge, on intellect. The knowledge they acquired was incomplete. By that choice they lost their way. They had been enjoying a blissful existence, living in harmony with all things. The partial knowledge they attained eating the fruit of the Tree of Knowledge brought to light a new, foreign perspective, a perception of division and separation.

Eating the fruit of the Tree of Knowledge dawned a new day, and gave rise to a new, limited consciousness. The ascent of that consciousness gave birth to mankind's nemesis, the ego. Man has struggled ever since, lost and misguided, enslaving himself to arrogance — the idea that by his intellect, by the mastery of knowledge, he might secure power. That fantasy led to the idea that by securing power man might master this life and become captain of his destiny. In this quest, mankind forfeits freedom and with it true peace and joy.

Original sin weighs heavy on every soul not because it is passed on as a birthright, but rather because it is embraced by the individual. We cling to false idols: the idols of money, fame, and power. This idolatry springs from a bankrupt idea — the belief that mankind is separate from what surrounds us and from what is. This belief conveyed through the story of Adam and Eve is captured in the language of the serpent: knowledge brings power. The powerful in turn harden in judgment and cling helplessly and hopelessly to experiences of this world. From this simple, yet far-reaching, belief, all pain and suffering spring.

The story of the fall of Adam holds lessons for us today. Adam is living a life of abundance in Paradise. All his needs are met, he enjoys abundance. He has with him the most beautiful woman on the face of the earth. He has but to do his part — to tend the Garden and live out his days frolicking in this playground. Yet he chooses a different way.

The character of Satan, the seed of discord, raises his voice through a serpent addressing the mother of mankind. The exchange recorded in the Book of Genesis is a narrative of the appeal and influence of the ego over humanity. The voice of what seems to be reason says man can have power; can be great; can take control.

Having control is a tempting premise. One we, with detached rationality, see now to be disastrous. How can someone who seems to have it all make such a simple mistake with eternal consequences? Ah, the folly of human nature. Yet we face the same temptation every day. Eve believes the serpent, not because of the logic of the serpent's argument, but rather because of the argument's appeal to her emotions, the intent of her desire to have more and be more, the fruit of the ego. A feeling I am familiar with, and one, I suppose, you recognize as well.

Knowledge is the most grievous veil between man and his Creator.

- Book of Certitude -

Together Adam and Eve eat of the fruit of the Tree of Knowledge. The man and woman disobey the Creator. For most people this ends the story of sin — sin was brought into the world by Adam and Eve's disobedience. From the simple act of eating fruit, the grandeur of the Garden fades into the bondage of pain and suffering for all mankind until the end of time.

Dim prospects, small hope in overwhelming despair. But this is not the end of the story. It is not even the end of the beginning of the story. Adam and Eve have another, more profound lesson to share.

The calamity, the tragedy of original sin, is not that Adam and Eve disobeyed the Creator. Adam and Eve got what they desired — power — the power to distinguish right from wrong. Their eating of the Tree of Knowledge elevated them to judge; it unleashed the ego. They chose to recognize a self, a me, separate from, and above, a higher authority.

Imagine living in a beautiful setting, warm and comfortable surrounded by great bounty — life is good. Existence is always and forever in the bliss of now. No yearning for yesterday, no anxiety about tomorrow, no concern today. What is, is. For the ego however, **everything** is not even close to enough. The ego has an insatiable desire for more: power, mastery, dominion. The ego seeks it all, for itself. The ego does not realize it is inseparable from the divine. In the quest to have it all, the ego moves us to defiance, to competition, to authority. Adam and Eve's original sin was not the act of disobedience; it was the indulgence of the ego. The woman considered and attempted to gain something she thought she did not have.

She coveted a false idol, power. What she secured instead was to set mankind on the path to wrestle lifetime after lifetime with an ego intent on leading us to pain and suffering.

When Adam and Eve's eyes were opened, they realized they were naked; they were ashamed. For the first time they saw

The punishment for demanding our own way is getting it.

themselves as separate from each other, separate from creation, and separate from the Creator. In one fell swoop they moved from actor to judge. The ego seized the intellect, they realized they were naked and they determined nakedness to be bad.

What sealed their fate, however, was not the Creator's judgment of them. The Creator knew they had eaten of the Tree. He offered a chance at redemption by questioning them. The responses they offered sealed their fate; they condemned themselves. The Creator asked Adam if he ate of the tree. Adam responded, "The woman made me do it." With his utterance, Adam failed to take responsibility for what he had done. The woman in turn, when questioned, pointed to the serpent as the culprit (true to our contemporary form), denying responsibility for her actions.

Original sin is not a ball and chain handed down to mankind through the generations from the original act of disobedience. What we know as "Original Sin" is a state of the human condition that we may either ignore or embrace, the force of the ego. We can master the ego or succumb to its intent and let the ego master us. Unfortunately most of us tend to believe it's not our choice — it's not our fault.

The story of creation in the Book of Genesis illustrates these points:

- Humanity's nature to covet is the work of the ego.
- The punishment for coveting is to get what we demand.
- We bind ourselves by consistently denying personal responsibility for the circumstances of our lives.

For our knowledge is imperfect
and our prophecy is imperfect;
but when the perfect comes,
the imperfect will pass away.
When I was a child, I spoke like a child,
I thought like a child,
I reasoned like a child;
when I became a man,
I gave up childish ways.
For now we see in a mirror dimly,
but then face to face.
Now I know in part;
then I shall understand fully.

- 1 CORINTHIANS -

Awareness and Ego

You Aren't What You Think...

If we were to run into each other on the street and I were to ask, "Who are you?" Your immediate reply would likely be your name. Consider for a moment: is your name you? Does it define you, in all your complexity, the depth of your desires, the range of your emotions, the strength of your convictions?

Does your name explain all the subtleties of who you are, where you have been, what you have done, and what you are about?

Not likely!

Your name is sound vibration, an utterance, a collection of letters written and spoken to conveniently label and identify the entity we call you — a human being defined in time and space.

Introductions are usually by name, sometimes by relationship (John's brother, Julie's sister, and so on). The next question most likely asked upon meeting is, "What do you do?" The reply normally offered is the person's most dominant or most important role, "I'm: an accountant, a truck driver, a teacher, I work at a factory, I sell real estate, I'm a doctor, a lawyer, a chimney sweep, a mom."

We routinely define people by the roles they play: mother, father, sister, brother, son, daughter. Then too we classify people by what they do: banker, baker, lawyer, doctor, seamstress, cook, soldier, actor, friend.

Are people really the roles they play? Do the roles we play define us completely and accurately?

Who are you? What do you do?

Does that label define you?

True wisdom is different from
much learning;
Much learning means little wisdom.

- TAO TE CHING -

Again, not likely!

Roles, like labels, are temporal descriptions defining a pattern of behavior. Labels are shorthand to help us relate, identify and categorize how we think about ourselves and others. We assume that labels simplify our thinking, simplify our relationships, and thereby simplify our lives.

Descriptive labels, like short, tall, fat, dumb, smart, popular, understanding, and wise, describe and define. Affixing a label ascribes certain traits and abilities to an individual. That label, however, ultimately serves to limit and restrict. We establish and accept labels out of convenience, to evoke a reaction or fix an impression of someone or of our selves. We accept labels as necessary language telling us what someone is, how they act, or what they are like.

In truth, however, labels rarely liberate. Instead they confine. Labels reveal more about the limits of one's thinking than about the individual the label attempts to define.

Though people constantly label and segregate others, many resist being defined by labels not of their own selection. People prefer to label themselves in ways that serve self image — in other words — ego. Sometimes this works out, sometimes not. This human relations shorthand of affixing labels only quickens people to judgment. People never fail to be amazed when someone escapes the box a label condemned them to.

Labels used to describe our selves, names, roles, attributes, or habits, do not accurately or adequately define us.

Now consider this: — Are you your thoughts?

Two plus two equals ____ (fill in the blank). Is the mathematical thought that is crossing your brain, you?

When you are sitting comfortably in your car, cruising down an abandoned stretch of highway, you can clearly distinguish between yourself and the sounds blaring from the radio. You would not say you are the music. Similarly in your own

Does not wisdom call out?
Does not understanding raise her voice?
On the heights along the way,
Where the paths meet, she takes her stand;
Beside the gates leading into the city
At the entrances, she cries aloud...

- Proverbs 8:1-3 -

mind, if you try, you can distinguish a you, from the sounds, images, language, and ideas that clutter and flit across your gray matter.

Relax for a moment and separate your thoughts from yourself.

Your thoughts, though intimately close, are separate from you.

The mind is a curious and wonderful gift; it functions much like a radio receiver. Thoughts dart across the mind like radio waves through space. You can scan various stations or in a split second tune to the station you desire by directing your focus. By harnessing attention you draw thoughts and ideas from the ethos (that reality, beyond perception, we agreed exists) to the experience of your time and place. Your mind translates ideas and the energy of will, from some other place, to the consciousness of here and now. As surely as you read these words you can separate a you from the noise and attention of thought.

So, again, are the thoughts you experience in your mind you? Do they define, explain, capture you, in all your shades of being? Are your thoughts you?

No! You are not your thoughts. You may internalize them, act on them, or animate them, or you may dismiss them altogether, but those ideas, images, and experiences introduced through what we commonly call thoughts, are not you.

Are you your emotions or feelings?

Those waves of energy that influence your body: fear, anger, sorrow, pain, joy, amazement, bewilderment, desire — are these you? The feelings and sensations that dominate, energize, and animate your body, are they you? Does any one emotion, literally "energy in motion," define you? Do all the emotional states you experience collectively define you? Do they absolutely determine what you do or how you act?

To you O men, I call out;
I raise my voice to all mankind,
You who are simple, gain prudence;
You who are foolish, gain understanding,
Listen, for I have worthy things to say,
I open my lips to speak what is right,
My mouth speaks what is true . . .

- Proverbs 8:4-7 -

No! Emotions and feelings are an aspect of your experience, they may influence actions and perceptions, but they are not you.

Pinch yourself. Yes, you are reading this right. Stop reading for just a moment, take two fingers and pinch your arm, your leg, your body somewhere. (If you feel frisky, pinch your significant other.) Do you feel a sensation of pressure, possibly pain? (There may be a delayed reaction when your significant other reacts and pinches you.)

Are you what you feel? Are you that tingling sensation of pressure on your body that you recognize and interpret in your mind?

Attempt for a moment to distinguish between the object of the sensation and the sensation itself, within your body. That sensation seems to be a part of you, but is it you?

Scientists categorize what we experience through touch as either heat or pressure, a difference in temperature or a force against our bodies. What we feel through the nervous system as the sense of touch may be generated from the external environment or originate from within. The heat or pressure we sense, however, is not us.

So, once again: are you what you feel, are you the sense of experiencing the environment? Do those sensations represent or define you completely?

No! Though another aspect of experience of physical reality, what you feel is not you.

What about the features of reality experienced through other senses — sight, sound, taste, or smell? As surely as we can define things that are not us, that are outside ourselves, we can come to discover what is us, what is self.

Start with the body. We can see our bodies. We feel, see, and experience the limits of the body. The definition of who and what we are must surely begin here. If you are not the labels

Choose my instruction instead of silver,
Wisdom rather than choice gold,
For wisdom is more precious than rubies,
And nothing you desire can compare with her.

- Proverbs 8:10-11 -

you affix, the roles you play, or your thoughts, emotions, or feelings, or even senses you experience, if you are none of these things — what then, are you?

Obviously, we are our bodies.

Well, are we?

Understanding this is an intellectual exercise. Consider for a moment: are you your body? Clearly, your body is a means to experience the physical reality of a time and place, but is it you? Where does your body start and stop? At your skin? The ends of your hair? Your lips? Your tongue? Your digestive tract? What if you lose an arm, or an eye, or an organ for that matter? What happens to you?

If our identity is our body, as the body changes our image of self changes as well. We recognize, deep in our being, a component of self that is enduring — not transient, but fixed. Up until the discussion of the body we have been considering the human being, the individual, from an experiential perspective. The body is our means to experience the environment here and now, but the body is not you. We experience energy through the body. Through our senses we capture the flow of energy from somewhere else into our locale, into our awareness. Through the body we gain awareness, we play out the drama of a time and place, but our essence is more profound than the body. Wisdom leads us to this realization.

Our True Essence— Pure Awareness

None of those aspects of experience just discussed are you. The you, the individual self, despite how cleverly it is clothed or disguised as something or someone, or how sophisticated its label, or how all-consuming its thoughts and feelings, your essence is pure awareness.

You, we, human beings are, at our core, awareness. We are observers of an earthly drama, dreamers of a grand dream.

You aren't what you think.

Thoughts, feelings, what you see, hear,
touch, taste or smell are not you.
You can't be defined by a label,
by possessions, by someone else.
The you that experiences defies explanation.

Despite all the trappings of this life, we each are individual portals observing, sensing, experiencing, the movement of energy in an infinite unfolding drama. **We are God's windows to this world.** Once we grasp this truth, accept it, and open ourselves to it, we release the chains of bondage and become free. The wisdom of this realization reunites us with all creation, with God.

The Self — Ego

We are what we are — **awareness/observer** — yet a challenging circumstance dominates our existence: we live what we think we are. The force moving us away from the realization of "self" as unencumbered observer frolicking in the playground, to the fearful and troubled submission to the ego (the snare of the human condition) is a mental miscalculation. The ego leads us from tranquility to turmoil — from abundance to competition and lack. Through fear and the overwhelming nature of the reality that surrounds us, we surrender to the illusion. We come to believe mankind is separate from the environment and individuals are separate from each other and separate from what is.

The **ego** is not, in and of itself, bad. Ego is that aspect of self that grounds awareness in time and space. It is the dimension of the human designed to allow him or her to immerse completely in the environment — in time, place, and circumstance. The ego is a necessary part of our experience. The ego is home to the survival mechanism, that part of the psyche that keeps us "in this world." The ego clings to the body and what the body can sense. It embraces physical reality, dismissing out of hand any alternative to what it can see, feel, and manipulate. The ego, though intended to be servant, seeks to be master. The ego is what makes the dream real. Unleashed, the ego intends to dominate; to define a separate self, a self apart and distinct from all else, a self that would be king.

If you aren't what you think,
What are you then?

You are something divine.
At your essence you are pure awareness —
a quiet observer.
You are a child of God.
Within you is the spirit of truth — find it!
Now is the only time — your time;
Your moment of truth — seize it!

The ego is a force of personality. Wayne Dyer, a spiritual teacher, sums ego up, expressed through six ideas:

1. I am what I have.
2. I am what I do.
3. I am my reputation.
4. I am separate from you.
5. I am separate from what is.
6. I am separate from God.

A Course in Miracles explains the power of these beliefs as, "We are asleep, dreaming that we are separate from God." That aspect of self that sees an "I" as separate, seeks to exalt that "I." The ego seeks to control, to dominate, and in so doing "be" something. By surrendering to the ego we lose contact with our essence, our awareness — and in so doing lose our freedom, and ultimately peace and joy.

As Eckhart Tolle, a spiritual teacher and author, states, "If you buy into the mental story of 'me,' your life may be reduced to the two-inch gap between the date of birth and the date of death on your tombstone. That dash represents the time and drama of your life."

Wisdom is embracing truth, the truth that the story is bigger than "me," bigger than "self," so much more than "ego" allows. Our true nature, as observer, as awareness, plays a role in the complex, ever unfolding, beautiful, exciting, never ending tale of creation, but still recognizes home is not here, and we have not left home.

As summarized by the pain or pleasure principle, creatures of all sorts act with two magnetic motivations: to increase pleasure or decrease pain. We seek to move toward pleasure and/or away from pain. This dynamic contrast similarly expresses wisdom. Wisdom operates in polarity (the duality of this reality). We act wisely by accepting truth and rejecting falsehood. The wise

For my lips detest wickedness.
All the words of my mouth are just;
None of them is crooked or perverse.
To the discerning all of them are right;
They are faultless to those who have insight.

- PROVERBS 8:7-9 -

accept the truth — we are aspects of the divine — and thereby move toward pleasure. The wise reject the ego — they refuse to submit to the idea of self as separate — and thereby move away from pain. Problems in life arise when people submit to the ego and fall prey to desires to dominate and control. Acceptance leads to peace and joy. Ego leads to pain and suffering.

The story, in all its dimensions, is grand, the truth far beyond comprehension. Though we may, by our own will, choose to act in the realm of domination and judgment, the grand plan will prevail. This is the paradox of life, the recognition of which is the influence of wisdom: we are small, some might say obscure, observers in a vast drama, yet at the same time we are part and parcel of the divine. Our aspect of divinity makes us responsible. We are observer and creator at the same time. Adam and Eve were comfortable in the Garden but by their wills they chose a different way. They chose to let separation dominate and have yet to accept responsibility for that choice.

The story is bigger than me. A "me," a "self," an "ego," only exists when we fail to recognize the truth. While the story is beyond us, we remain the author. The final outcome is in our hands.

Recognizing Our True Nature

Some power greater than self animates this existence; that power has brought us to the crossroads of energy and intention — life. For our part, we are that still watcher — the observer — taking in the experience; feeling the emotions, living the outcome of choices. We navigate the environment and, as we are aspects of the divine, have a hand in creating the experience. The circumstances and the environment are both ultimately of our own creation. We are not separate from what is, but rather one with what is.

What sustains, energizes and moves us through life is unifying spirit. Joy in this journey is not found in grasping, seizing

Wisdom is — complete self-responsibility with complete surrender.

- GARY ZUKAV -

the illusion, the tangible pieces of experience (as pleasurable or painful as they may seem). Rather, wisdom is realized by accepting the journey for what it is — an extremely diverse, sometimes thrilling, sometimes bewildering, always wildly engaging ride.

We, at our core, are something more, something outside the realm of "physical reality" at home in, and from, some other reality. This ultimate reality is beyond our five senses; it is beyond intellect and reason; it is the realm of spirit. Though we experience aspects of, and recognize ultimate reality in, all we see, feel, and do, we can know our true selves and ultimate reality only through the still spirit of the observer, our higher selves.

Deep down inside, we recognize something beyond this time and space. If we listen, if we are open, we begin to bring into our awareness the idea we are part of something greater. Though the ego says we are separate, we sense we are part of the whole — we yearn to be whole.

Reduced to its simplest measure, wisdom is understanding that we have but one choice, a choice between freedom or bondage. Freedom is accepting the lessons of life, and the wisdom of creation. Bondage is empowering the ego and resisting life. Our choice is either to accept or resist. We have power when we realize everything that exists outside and around our selves is the product of that choice, and is of our making. Only when we assume complete responsibility for our lives can we experience complete freedom.

We can propagate original sin, like Adam and Eve, by succumbing to the lure of the ego or we can accept responsibility, reject the ego and listen to that still, small voice inside guiding us and telling us that the way is easy, the burden is light. **Humility empowers our true nature and is the way to wisdom.**

I, wisdom, dwell together with prudence;
I possess knowledge and discretion.
To fear the Lord is to hate evil,
I hate pride and arrogance,
Evil behavior and perverse speech.
Counsel and sound judgment are mine;
I have understanding and power.

- Proverbs 8:12-14 -

Wisdom to accept; to find your way

✦ **Our true nature: observer.** ✦

✦ **We are not separate.** ✦

✦ **We are responsible.** ✦

✦ **We have a choice.** ✦

Our true nature is not of this world. We are observers in a foreign land, a playground or a nightmare of our own design. Though we are small elements of a grand scheme, we have a measure of power over our circumstances if we see past the illusion and grasp the truth. All God's creatures are windows on the world, immersed in, reveling in creation. As observers human beings fulfill a purpose for the Creator. We each experience a unique drama with a unique purpose — a purpose beyond intellect.

The essence of being is awareness. And only humans, at least as far as we have discovered, have been given the gift of consciousness that recognizes awareness.

While we possess facets beyond imagining and power beyond measure, we often act like a monkey caught with its paw in a jar, holding tight to a prize; we imprison ourselves. By way of a corrupt idea of being more by having more, the ego seeks and secures dominion. The parents of the human family, Adam and Eve in the Bible's creation story, did not accept what they had — with profound consequences. They coveted, they chose, they acted. And still today, we compound the error by denying responsibility for our circumstances and our actions.

The ego is that part of self that defines a me and craves control. The ego seeks to rule and, it believes, by so doing secure its immortality. The folly of humans is yielding to the beguiling message of ego. The ego can be a useful tool allowing individuals a vantage point on the ride of life. However, instead of controlling the tool, humans submit to its will — allowing the servant to be the master.

Now then, my people, listen to me;
Blessed are those who keep my ways.
Listen to my instruction and be wise;
Do not ignore it.
Blessed is the man who listens to me,
Watching daily at my doors,
Waiting at my doorway.
For whoever finds me finds life
And receives favor from the Lord.
But whoever rails to find me harms himself;
All who hate me love death.

- PROVERBS 8:32-36 -

To seal our fate, if things do not go as we hope, as we desire, or as we demand, we blame someone or something else. We refuse to take responsibility for our life circumstances and for what we ultimately control — reactions to experiences and the choices those experiences engender.

Wisdom says we have but one choice: a choice between freedom and bondage. Freedom is the way of peace, love, and joy. Bondage, the way of ego, leads to despair.

Though we find ourselves immersed in a story, a story rich with color and texture, character and potential, wisdom allows us to realize we are both actors in and co-creators of the drama. We are responsible observers. As elements of the Creator's awareness, we watch and experience the unfolding kaleidoscope of life. As fully divine aspects of the whole we are responsible for the drama that unfolds. A paradox it seems.

Ultimately, man is not master of his destiny, a collective force far greater is. Yet man is one with the power of the divine. Every feeling, every choice, every action contributes to the whole. Every human, every creature, every aspect of this world is a part of the whole. We are connected and responsible, one for the other. Wisdom leads us to recognize and embrace this truth, a truth that leads to a fuller, happier, freer life.

The first and most profound choice to secure the blessings of wisdom is to choose opportunity over ego. When humans release themselves from the grip of the ego they find peace and joy unparalleled in the forest of the illusion. Our first choice must be to move away from pain. We are destined to repeat the lesson until we learn that ego (the dominance of self) leads to pain. As actors in (observers), and co-creators of (responsible for) this unfolding adventure, we command a body, a mind, and a will. We can employ these faculties within an environment, in rhythm with a greater symphony, to a defined and determined end.

There is no more to wisdom than this:
Accept the grace of God.

By surrendering to the influence of the ego, a simple act of resistance leads us out of the moment, out of the experience and the acceptance of what is. The ego, that aspect of the body, mind, and will that seeks to dominate, belabors the past and offers hope in a tangible future all the while looking for, longing for, a time and circumstance to dominate — a time when ego will take charge, take control. Eating of the fruit of the Tree of Knowledge is a metaphor not for an act thousands of years ago but rather for the reality of our contemporary struggle, the ongoing struggle of humanity with ego.

Through ego's quest we get lost in the illusion and miss the thrill of the good life intended for us to experience.

Adam and Eve embraced the deception of the ego and denied any responsibility in doing so. To not fall in the same trap, to realize freedom and peace, we must not allow the ego to dominate our lives. We must accept who we are, what we are, and the circumstances of our existence. We must recognize our culpability in those circumstances. Only by heeding wisdom's soft call will we recognize we are watching "B-grade" movies all the while with the remote control in hand. We can choose to change the channel.

The earth plane, this world, is constant motion. Life is the convergence of idea energy. We, each and every one of us, contribute to the epic. Ideas manifest through our choices, our actions, our very beings. The motion, the journey experienced as life, is the constant ebb and flow of ideas harnessing energy and manifesting experience.

Only by our ultimate acceptance of life in the present will we shake the serpent. We are ultimately responsible. The ego is not in charge. We cannot allow the ego control. Until we accept full responsibility for what we have, are, and do will we understand what the ego tells us about being separate is a lie. Embrace wisdom, live the paradox, accept responsibility for what seems beyond our control.

Beyond intellect is truth.
Living that truth is embracing wisdom.

We provide an individual perspective and experience of this existence, but we are not separate, nor alone in it. By embracing the paradox, denying self and accepting full and total responsibility for the quality of our experience, we liberate our selves. Wisdom leads us to the fulfillment of pure love and the connection of pure bliss. Through wisdom we realize, no matter what happens we are at home, we are safe, and we are whole — we are one.

Know the truth and the truth will set you free.

Pray for wisdom.
If you are wise, your life will be full. . .

Courage

to Go
to Act
to Let Go

There is no greater gift than to lay down one's life for one's friends.
- JOHN 15:13 -

The kingdom of God is at hand.

The day was a day like any other — the sun shone bright, a light breeze offered respite from the summer heat, the work of living carried on. In some other place, at some other time, this day would have been considered a day of beauty and opportunity but not in this place, not at this time. The only opportunity offered here, this day, was an opportunity for suffering and sacrifice. This was a place like no other, in an era of darkness, where fear and hatred dominated. The work of killing and the process of dying were raised to art forms of the most egregious kind. The place was Auschwitz, the time, late July 1941. Hitler's dream of the Third Reich, a new world order dominated by Nazi ideals, empowered by a pure, noble race, was coming together in its most grotesque fashion — at death camps, places where brutality and inhumanity knew no bounds.

Far from the war front, far from the mighty armies' crusade for political domination, waged a simple struggle, a fight for survival, a battle for human dignity, engaged in on a personal scale. Despite the forces of oppression and the hatred brought to bear on a defenseless people, a light continued to shimmer, a glimmer of hope, of trust and of faith, an undying, uncompromising love, the cornerstone of one man's life, an inspiration in courage.

On this day Maximillian Maria Kolbe stepped forward to silently offer his life in exchange for the life of another.

Prisoner 16770, Maximillian Maria Kolbe, had found his way to hell on earth by means of his devotion to truth. As a Franciscan priest, Maximillian had committed his life to spreading the Gospel, the Good News, through his missionary work and notably through his publishing house. It was the publishing house that had brought him to the attention of the Gestapo.

As a young man Maximillian had had aspirations of becoming a scientist. He dismissed the idea of a career in science considering instead the vocation of noble warrior, defender of Poland. In the end, however, rather than enlisting in the Army he answered a stronger calling. He became a spiritual soldier, a man of focused energy and ability helping people find their way in a sometimes bewildering, often lonely, and frightening world.

Maximillian's zeal, vision, and energy moved him around the globe. He traveled abroad doing missionary work in India and Japan. Closer to home, he established an evangelization center near Warsaw called Niepokalanow, the "City of the Immaculata." By 1938, the City had expanded from 18 friars to an incredible 650, making it the largest Catholic religious house in the world.

Maximillian was an unimposing figure, of medium build; what he lacked in stature he made up for in enthusiasm and optimism. His eyes shone with the promise of life even as his intellect wrestled with the forces of evil in the world. Maximillian was humble and kind, displaying a spark of conviction that brought him the trust and admiration of those he came in contact with. He was a man of contrasts in a world that considered appearance, power, and position all that mattered. He was intent on spreading the truth the best way he could. That truth dismissed the ideas of living dedicated to anything but the most uncompromised conviction that life was solely for the glory of God expressed through unwavering love.

In his effort to reach more people, Maximillian planned to start a printing house where information could be mass produced and sent to millions. When he conceived the idea, he had only half of the necessary funds. He trusted and prayed, and miraculously the funds he needed quickly appeared.

With the assistance of other priests and religious, Maximillian developed a monthly magazine with a circulation of more than one million, and a daily newspaper with a circulation of 230,000. The publishing house produced countless inspirational and devotional tracts as well. The friars used the latest printing and administrative technologies to turn out their publications and reach the masses.

An innovator and visionary, Maximillian also started a radio station and planned to build a motion picture studio. All of this was used for and intended to teach the whole world, spreading hope and faith through the example and living power of a humble Jew who had walked the earth two thousand years before.

In a Poland controlled by Nazis, Maximillian's religious community inevitably came under suspicion. The Nazi secret police watched closely. In particular, the printing apostolate Maximillian had started was a target of Nazi hatred. Finally, emboldened by their apparent successes and leveraging their dominion over the local populace, the Nazis closed the friary down.

Maximillian was initially arrested by the Gestapo and released in December 1939. In February 1941, he was arrested again and imprisoned in Warsaw. While in Warsaw he suffered from an inflammation of the lungs and was confined to the infirmary. Though ill, he carried on his priestly work surreptitiously, hearing confessions in unlikely places and ministering to those around him, prisoners and captors alike, by way of his loving example. On May 28, 1941, Maximillian, in a group of 320 prisoners, was transferred to the concentration camp at Auschwitz.

Auschwitz, the largest mass-murder site in the history of the world, did not start out as a death camp. By order of Reichsfuhrer SS Heinrich Himmler, on 27 April 1940, Rudolf Höss, a captain in the SS, was to establish a camp at the southwestern Polish town of Oswiecim primarily to confine and oppress Polish dissidents whom the Nazis considered to be a threat to their occupation. As Höss wrote in his memoirs, prior to his execution, "The task wasn't easy. In the shortest possible time, I had to create a camp for 10,000 prisoners using the existing complex of buildings which were well constructed but were completely run down and swarming with vermin."

Oswiecim was situated on major railroad lines. The surrounding area was rich in natural resources, particularly fresh water, lime, and coal. This made it an excellent location for a factory to manufacture war materials. A dream of Nazi leaders was that the factory would fund the creation of a model Nazi settlement where Auschwitz prisoners would work as slave laborers and the SS would profit by selling coal and gravel as well as labor.

Toward the end of 1940, the Nazis determined to triple Auschwitz's capacity from 10,000 to 30,000 prisoners. Auschwitz would be a backwater no longer; it would become the largest concentration camp in the Nazi empire.

Höss' belief was that true opponents of the state had to be securely locked up. And to accomplish the task required extraordinary toughness. He admitted that Auschwitz was a concentration camp where cruel and brutal treatment was routine. Eventually, his efforts led to extermination on an industrial scale with some estimates running as high as three million persons killed through gassing, starvation, disease, shooting, and burning.

The camp buildings were nondescript: two-story gray brick and single-story dull wood. Laid out neatly in rows, simplicity, conformity, and unity characterized the military settlement. The grounds were devoid of life: brown dirt, sand and gravel offered no sustenance for mind or body. Watchtowers were built at strategic points along the chain-link and barbed-wire fence. The watchtowers were not designed so much to protect the camp from intruders as they were to ensure the guests never checked out. A few old trees, unaffected by the human struggle, stood watch on the outskirts of the camp like stooped sentinels over the macabre scene. The wrought-iron gate welcomed new arrivals with the words: *Arbeit Macht Frei* (Work Makes You Free).

Maximillian, along with hundreds of fellow prisoners, unloaded at the railway ramp, the goods station. The weary travelers, exhausted and anxious, were not sure what lie ahead and remained suspicious of the menacing Nazis' intentions. A survivor describes a typical arrival:

For those new arrivals to the camp, as we stood, waiting for instructions, we watched. Two groups of strange individuals emerged into the light of the lamps. They walked in squads, in rows of three, with an odd, embarrassed step, head dangling in front, arms rigid. On their heads, they wore comic berets and were all dressed in long striped overcoats, which even by night and from a distance looked filthy and in rags. They walked in a large circle around us, never drawing near, and in silence began to busy themselves with our luggage and to climb in and out of the empty wagons.

We looked at each other without a word. It was all incomprehensible and mad, but one thing we had understood. This was the metamorphosis that awaited us. Tomorrow we would be like them.[3a]

The prisoners immediately realized, from their very first contacts with the contemptuous men with the black patches, that knowing or not knowing German was a watershed. Those who understood them and answered in an articulate manner could establish the semblance of a human relationship. To those who did not understand, the menacing soldiers reacted in a manner that astonished and frightened — an order that had been pronounced in the calm voice of a man who knows he will be obeyed was repeated word for word in a loud, angry voice, then screamed at the top of his lungs as if he were addressing a deaf person or indeed a domestic animal, more responsive to the tone than the content of the message.

If anyone hesitated (and everyone hesitated because they did not understand and were terrorized) the blows fell, and it was obvious that they were a variant of the same language — use of the word to communicate thought, this necessary and sufficient mechanism for man to be man, had fallen into disuse. This was a signal — those people were no longer men.[3b]

One prisoner recalled the indignity that was commonplace:

> *In this place it is practically pointless to wash every day in the turbid water of the filthy washbasins for purposes of cleanliness and health; but it is most important as a symbol of remaining vitality, and necessary as an instrument of moral survival.*
>
> *I must confess it: after only one week of prison, the instinct for cleanliness disappeared in me. I wander aimlessly around the washroom when I suddenly see Steinlauf, my friend aged almost fifty, with nude torso, scrub his neck and shoulders with little success (he has no soap) but great energy. Steinlauf sees me and greets me, and with great energy asks me why I do not wash. Why should I wash? Would I be better off than I am? Would I please someone more? Would I live a day, an hour longer? I would probably live a shorter time, because to wash is an effort, a waste of energy and warmth. Does not Steinlauf know that after half an hour with the coal sacks every difference between him and me will have disappeared?... But this was the sense, not forgotten either then or later: that precisely because this was a great machine to reduce us to beasts, we must not become beasts; that even in this place one can survive, and therefore one must want to survive, to tell the story, to bear witness; and that to survive we must force ourselves to save at least the skeleton, the scaffolding, the form of civilization. We are slaves, deprived of every right, exposed to every insult, condemned to certain death, but we still possess one power, and we must defend it with all our strength for it is the last — the power to refuse our consent. So we must certainly wash our faces without soap in dirty water and dry ourselves on our jackets.*[3c]

The average life expectancy at Auschwitz was a few months. The meager rations, hard work, and brutal treatment took their toll. Lucie Adelsberger describes the life of the children: "Like the adults, the kids were only a mere bag of bones, without muscles or fat — with thin skin scrubbed through and through beyond the hard bones of the skeleton, ignited to ulcerated wounds. Sores covered the underfed body from the top to the bottom and thus deprived it from the last rest of energy. Abscesses deeply gnawed the mouth, hollowed out the jaw and perforated the cheeks like cancer. Many decaying bodies were full of water because of the burning hunger; they swelled to shapeless bulks which could not move anymore. Diarrhea, lasting for weeks, dissolved their irresistant bodies until nothing remained ..."

Into this scene stepped hope: Maximillian resumed his missionary work. As the prisoners were slowly and systematically starved, when food was brought, everyone struggled to get his place and be sure of a portion. Maximillian, however, stood aside in spite of the ravages of hunger. Frequently there would be none left for him. At other times he shared his meager ration of soup or bread with others who were famished.

To illustrate the challenge of holding onto life by a thread, another prisoner recorded a scene of desperation, exertion, and finally exhaustion; a scene played out daily in Auschwitz. In this case a man would trade his last breath for a meager taste of squalid soup.

With the war raging, air raid warnings were common events at military camps, including detention camps like Auschwitz. Never knowing whether an air raid warning was a drill or the signal of an actual attack, tensions always ran high for prisoners and guards alike. As the sirens sounded, guards scurried to their designated fighting positions intent on fending off any would-be intruder. The prisoners assembled as they were directed and drilled to do. Their lives were of no value, so standing in the open during an air raid was of little consequence.

On this occasion, however, as the guards and staff scurried about, and with hundreds of prisoners looking on, one lone, nearly starved prisoner spotted an opportunity and acted to capitalize on it. This ghost of a man, desperate for nourishment, spied a caldron of steaming hot soup temporarily abandoned near the kitchen.

Instead of taking his designated place among the condemned, this man made his way from his barracks on his belly, inch by inch, toward the coveted prize. The other prisoners, as malnourished and pained, stood in awe, watching silently, with both compassion and contempt — compassion for his need, and contempt for his daring. Though hope traveled with him, this was a feat the prisoners in formation could not duplicate. They were watching a man commit suicide for steaming, putrid broth.

The man scraped and scratched his way to the boiling pot. With every last ounce of strength his feeble body could muster, he hoisted himself up to the caldron's rim. He gazed with longing and satisfaction at the object of his triumph. He pondered his reflection, then lunged for his prize. His exertion exploded in a crash. The startled prisoners watched as the man writhed in pain, but only for an instant, then he settled in the peace of death to struggle no more.[3d]

Maximillian continued his practice of secretly hearing confessions and holding Mass for others in the camp. His work for the faith, even under these terrible conditions, endured. He would comfort the prisoners, saying, "Hate is not creative. Our sorrow is necessary that those who live after us may be happy."

Maximillian would plead with the prisoners to forgive their persecutors and overcome evil with good. Over the course of the months at Auschwitz he ministered to the needy and offered hope to those slipping into hopelessness. His captors were not pleased with his kindness and beat him at every opportunity to break his spirit and demonstrate their power. Maximillian recognized the fear and arrogance manifested by his captors attacks as veils of ignorance; they were lost in an illusion, struggling through violence, to lift themselves up. Every lash of a tongue and every sting of a fist reminded Maximillian of the words Jesus offered: "Forgive them, for they know not what they do."

Despite endless privation and countless beatings Maximillian persisted in courage, determined to offer kindness to people whose sense of decency had been all but shattered.

A camp doctor who treated the patients in Maximillian's block, Block Twelve, said that Maximillian would not let himself be treated before any other prisoners in that block. He sacrificed himself for the other prisoners.

Maximillian attempted to live what he had written: "No one in the world can change truth. What we can do and should do is seek it and serve it when it is found. The real conflict is inner conflict. Beyond armies of occupation and the catacombs of concentration camps, there are two irreconcilable enemies in the depth of every soul: good and evil, sin and love. And what use are victories on the battlefield if we ourselves are defeated in our innermost personal selves?"

On this day in late July a prisoner had escaped. At Auschwitz the camp's rule, in order to discourage escapes, was that if one prisoner got away, ten died in his place. Once the guards discovered a prisoner was missing, all the men from the escaped prisoner's block were made to stand in the sun without food and water. Weak from malnutrition and physical abuse, the men stood quietly, each alone in his own thoughts.

As they stood, watching and waiting the camp's first officer, Karl Fritsch, approached. Fritsch was not to be crossed. He was a man whose ego overcame any objection to systematic discipline followed by systematic death. He had no use for compassion and little use for the prisoners, whom he considered animals, before him. Their purpose was to produce for him. He was, in many ways the cause of their plight and ultimately indifferent to their deaths. Fritsch, at the time of his encounter with Maximillian, was at work devising a more efficient and effective way of disposing of what he considered the vermin populating the camp. Fritsch soon refined his methods by gassing 850 malnourished and ill prisoners. He established mass murder as a daily routine.

"The fugitive has not been found!" Fritsch screamed. "Ten of you will die for him in the starvation bunker."

Hope lingered like a withering leaf but was not yet dead at Auschwitz. Though many had died at the hands of their Nazi captors, the faint possibility of freedom still animated a troubled existence. The task was to survive the tribulations. Hope lay outside the wire — beyond the towers, away from the violence and hatred. Still there were two ways out: the first, through the crematorium; the second, through the gate.

The prisoners trembled in anticipation of whom would be chosen. A few days in the bunker without food and water, and a man's innards dry up, and his brain turns to fire.

At Fritsch's direction, a guard forebodingly called out the names of 10 men who were to die in the escaped prisoner's place. One by one, the names were read — the condemned segregated from the group. For now, as the prisoners had done too many times to remember, they stood numb with dread. Polish Army Sergeant Francis Gajowniczek imprisoned for helping the Polish Resistance, was stung by the weight of the sound of his name. He cried out, "Have mercy! I have a wife and children." But mercy was a commodity in short supply. First Officer Fritsch had no cause for leniency.

Into the gap between life and death stepped Maximillian Kolbe. He shuffled forward, unassuming and silent, his body ravaged by abuse, weak from deprivation; he was a pathetic, scrawny sight. He stood dirty, tired, hungry, and frail; illness and indignity had been his lot these many months, a fate he never embraced. Standing humbly before Fritsch, Maximillian's presence defined a contrast, bringing a sense of grace and dignity, an unseen power, to the horrific drama.

The sight of Maximillian and the gravity of this gesture caused Fritsch pause. Captivated and awed by the unseen force, Fritsch stared at the pathetic sight. Maximillian offered, "I am a Catholic priest from Poland; I would like to take his place, because he has a wife and children."

Astounded and amazed at what he had heard, the Nazi barked, "What does this Polish pig want?"

Maximillian pointed with his hand to the condemned Francis Gajowniczek and repeated "I am a Catholic priest from Poland; I would like to take his place, because he has a wife and children."

The other prisoners, standing by, relieved their names had not been called, watched in horror, believing that Fritsch would be angered and would refuse the request, or would order the death of both men. Fritsch remained silent for a moment. What his thoughts were on being confronted by this brave, humble man we can only speculate about. Amazingly, however, he acceded to the request. Apparently the Nazis had more use for a younger worker than for an older one, and were happy to make the exchange. Francis Gajowniczek was returned to the ranks, and Maximillian took his place.

The dreadful irony of the story is that the "escaped prisoner" was later found drowned in a camp latrine, so the terrible reprisal was exercised without cause.

Maximillian was hurled down the stairs of Building 13 along with the other victims and simply left there to starve. We know some of the details of his last days because the guard who kept the records was so impressed with Maximillian he took precise notes.

During those waning days, Maximillian led the victims in hymns and prayer. When he became too weak to speak aloud, he whispered his prayers. After two weeks, only four of the 10 were still alive. The guards, needing the space for more prisoners, decided to hasten the deaths with lethal doses of carbolic acid. Maximillian alone was completely conscious. One by one, without pause or ceremony, each breathing man was injected with poison. Maximilian was last. One of the most heroic acts of the twentieth century reached its conclusion on that day, August 14, 1941, when the Franciscan friar, Maximillian Kolbe, weak though he was, raised his arm to receive the lethal injection of carbolic acid, triumphantly embracing martyrdom.[3e]

Maximillian's final act of courage and faith demonstrates a sentiment expressed poignantly in a note, a final prayer, found by the body of a dead child upon the liberation of another death camp, Ravens Brook, at the end of the war:

Oh Lord, remember not only the men and women of good will, but also those of ill will. But do not remember the suffering they inflicted on us, remember the fruits we have bought. Thanks to this suffering — our comradeship, our loyalty, our humanity, our courage, our generosity, the greatness of heart which has grown out of all of this — when they come to judgment let all the fruits we have borne be their forgiveness.

Pope John Paul II spoke of Maximillian:

What happened in the starvation bunker in the concentration camp at Oswiecim (Auschwitz) on August 14, 1941?

The reply is given in today's liturgy. "God tested" Maximillian Maria "and found him worthy of himself" (Wisdom 3:5). God tested him "like gold in the furnace and like a sacrificial burnt offering he accepted him" (Wisdom 3:6). Even if "in the sight of men he was punished," yet "his

No greater gift than to lay down one's life for one's friends.

- JOHN 15:13 -

> *hope is full of immortality." For "the souls of the righteous are in the hands of God and no torment will ever touch them." And when — humanly speaking — torment and death came to them, when "in the eyes of men they seemed to have died..." when "their departure from us was thought to be an affliction...," "they are in peace." They experience life and glory "in the hands of God" (Wisdom 3:1–4).*
>
> *There were fulfilled the words spoken by Christ to the Apostles that they "should go and bear fruit and that their fruit should abide" (John 15:16).*

Maximillian's extraordinary act and his extraordinary behavior under the most trying circumstances is a living testament, a living example of what is possible if we are willing to dismiss discomfort, humbly accept the circumstances of life, good or bad, and instead courageously focus on the joy of being.

Maximillian did not have a highly developed tolerance for pain. His body, senses, emotions were no less receptive. He did have something most of us long for but still cannot find: a sense of purpose, a sense of faith, and the courage to act on those convictions. Maximillian was not without an ego, but he was able to overcome it and act freely. His actions were wise beyond human comprehension. He expressed courage daily as he chose to loosen the bonds of the physical life, not clinging to time or circumstance or feeling. Rather he moved forward, giving where he could, and finding joy and peace at every turn. No matter where he was or what appeared to whirl about him something enduring, something powerful, something wise grounded his core. Maximillian discovered that peace and joy were within — all he had to do was stop clinging to the world to find his way home.

To conquer fear
is the beginning of wisdom.

- Bertrand Russell -

Face Fear

What Are We Afraid Of?

What is it you fear?

Death?
Public speaking?
Conflict?
Loss of control?
Loss of power?
Loss of esteem?
Discomfort?
Illness?
Pain?
The unknown?

Generally, we recognize fear as a negative, disempowering emotion. The energy fear exerts, the impact of fear gripping our bodies, amounts to stress — physical, emotional, psychological. Fear is wholly and entirely experienced in the body (the physical body by way of a reaction in the brain). We produce, accept, invite in, the emotion of fear through the interpretation of sensory perceptions — that is, through judging the circumstances we perceive— by projecting into the future. These mental projections may be tangible — localized in time and space, plausible, inevitable, or imagined. Courage is the ability to sort through the perceptions, in an instant or over time, and realize the actual gravity of the event relative to the true and enduring nature of the spirit.

Lots of words to say: courage recognizes what matters, and when it comes to fear, most things don't.

We broadly distinguish between two types of fear: physical (a threat to the body and/or existence); or emotional (a threat to

Love has no room for fear; rather,
Perfect love casts out all fear . . .
Love is not perfect in one who is afraid.

- JOHN 1:18 -

psychological status and/or expectations). With physical fear, energy erupts from the body's sensing of a threat (potential for pain). With emotional fear, the body generates energy by a construct of the mind. In both cases, if not checked, our minds actually accelerate the energy of fear. Fear of physical pain is closely linked to our survival mechanism. Fear generated from risk of loss is closely aligned to expectations for the future.

Fear disempowers, but its outcome — that is, the circumstances resulting from the motivation of fear — need not always be negative. Here is a simple example: we have a natural fear of heights; the sensation of fear cautions us when getting too close to the edge, keeping us from a fall. Fear energy can generate a powerful motivation for positive action. It can be a signal to act. Fear, however, is always a stressor. Emotional fear often misguides and always limits. Fear wears on the mind and body and, over time, drains it of strength. Fear is one of the most powerful tools of the ego, keeping us from peace and joy. Fear originates from one source — our clinging nature.

Fear is from the Ego

Our experience of this life, in a simple phrase, is awareness perceiving energy. The drama of everyday existence is our interaction with, interpretation and manipulation of, localized energy. Fear is a type of energy, energy that we empower, energy we invite in, energy we generate.

Fear originates from the ego, that part of "self" that is of the world, the instinct, the intellect that says, "I am separate, alone, and in competition to survive."

The ego generates fear for practical "survival" reasons, but also to ensure dominion. The ego ushers in fear to define a drama, to create conflict, to color the experience. Fear is not a force outside our selves, fear is the power of the mind, of the

Nothing external has any power over you.

- Ralph Waldo Emerson -

ego. As the ego takes over consciousness it dominates, limits, and controls. With fear we can never be free. But our bondage is self induced. We create the very emotion, the energy, limiting us. Fear is not from "out there"; fear is from within.

Ultimate Fear

To experience fear we must have a sense of risk, the possibility of loss. The question is, what have we got to lose? Our projection into the future suggests we are going to lose something. First consider: what do we have?

In this reality, in this society we make a big deal about rights of ownership, but what does owning mean? At best we are temporary caretakers of things that come into our awareness: our bodies, relationships, the environment and a host of objects we like to call possessions. When we lay claim to an object, defining it as ours, we fall prey to the ego. Our essence needs to possess nothing. In essence we need nothing. We are one with all things, yet our person, the identity we characterize as "me," through the ego, seeks surety by way of ownership, through "my".

When we fall victim to the whims of the ego we put ourselves on a quest to possess ever more. Once on the hunt, we are lost, wandering aimlessly. We really have nothing to lose.

By attaching ourselves to objects, or attributes, or ideas about ourselves and reality, we set the conditions for fear. Fear can exist only in concert with a sense of loss of some aspect of identity — the idea of who we are — with its inherent baggage (physical body, roles, possessions, abilities, status, and so on). Fear can exist only when we lose our sense of spiritual connection and permanence and succumb to the illusion of object reality. Fear arises when we separate ourselves from the source, find ourselves alone, detached, and competing for survival.

True freedom is to risk nothing.
In truth, you have nothing to lose.

To be free, have the courage to let go.

A fundamental fear is the fear of loss of identity. A universal example, though for many not the ultimate fear, is the fear of death. The fear of death may not be the definitive example of a fear of loss because some people dread other aspects of a loss of identity more — loss of status, loss of esteem, loss of relationship. However, we humans have within us, closely linked to what is defined as ego, a survival instinct. This instinct is an aspect of being that is our most basic motivation. Lost in the labyrinth of the world, we seek to survive. Survival is a core "rule of the game". So we all recognize in ourselves, those of us that are less spiritually connected, a fear of death.

What we fear the most about death is that "I" (an identity) may no longer exist. Death is an unknown, a condition, a puzzle the intellect struggles to solve. At best the intellect settles on a comforting rationalization for temporary solace.

Besides the idea of death itself, the end of identity, we also fear the journey. We fear the process of dying, the expectation of discomfort at best, and downright pain at worst. The question of loss, entangled with the concept of self (body, roles, attributes, intentions), translates into, what happens to "me"?

Death for most of us, is the ultimate personal dilemma. Our lives are marked by two inescapable events: birth and death. We made it through the first event; birth is now in the past. The other inescapable event waits around the bend, somewhere up ahead. Luckily, most people (except those confronted with illness or extreme circumstances) don't hold in mind a concept of departure from life around the very next turn. Usually the event is held in abeyance to be considered and dealt with at some later date. However, if circumstances arise — a slip at the top of the stairs, an oncoming automobile, a threatening situation coming into our awareness — we appreciate that death is closer than we thought.

The challenge death poses for our concept of self, characterized another way, is: What happens to me, my identity, my ego,

The courage we desire and
prize we seek is not the
courage to die decently,
but to live fully.

- Thomas Carlyle -

the "me" I have grown so fond of, so attached to, the entity, the person, body, roles, attributes I have come to know and love?

Who knows?

Without question, there is life after death. We observe "life after death" all around us every day. Plants, animals, systems, and people die, and yet life goes on. Life doesn't stop; the cycle of life continues. The circumstance of death for plants, animals and other people though, is somehow different than the personal death of "me".

Consider for a moment, this world — life as you know it — without you. Will life go on? Does it, would it matter? We find ourselves again arriving at a paradox. Presumably we are an insignificant speck, a marginal player relative to the vastness of the universe and the scale of eternity. Our entire lives and everything we touch and influence would not even register a blip on the scope of time and space. Intellectually we may understand this comparison but emotionally we can never accept its implication. Our being screams to be somebody. The being we define as "self" is everything. The separate and distinct being, characterized by ego, that inhabits this slice of time and space yearns for immortality, yearns for importance.

The truth is, we are immortal. We are spirits on a magical adventure temporarily bound by time and space and circumstance. We came here of our own choosing, for our own purpose. We are still one with all that is, whole and complete with limitless potential. We are the creators of the limitations we face and capable of unleashing their restraints. But I digress…

Back to our question: does my life continue after death? If I accept another reality — other than that perceived through my five senses — what will become of "me"? Will "I" exist when my body quits? This question rattles the ego to the bone. If there is no "me", does anything matter? I am trapped and powerless to keep myself alive.

A Psalm of Life

Tell me not, in mournful numbers,
Life is but an empty dream!
For the soul is dead that slumbers,
And things are not what they seem.

Life is real! Life is earnest!
And the grave is not its goal;
Dust thou are, to dust returnest,
Was not spoken of the soul.

- HENRY WADSWORTH LONGFELLOW -

Returning to those three options proposed earlier about who we are, consider these alternatives as to what happens upon death:

1. When the body ceases to function, or in other words, dies, the life, or consciousness within, ceases to exist. It is no more — it is kaput, fini, terminated.
2. When the body dies the life force that animates it dissolves or merges back into the essence from which it came. It has no identity, no "me".
3. When the body ceases to exist, life in this physical reality ends. However, the personal life force, an identity, moves to a new dimension, a new place and experiences a new, different reality.

The intellect and the ego will never settle this question. The mystery, by design, is too great to fathom. The prospect we face, of potentially losing "me", however, is nearly unbearable. The struggle of the intellect, the strain of the ego to solve the mystery binds us to the journey, makes us vulnerable to fear. The ego, seeking conflict, is enraptured by the mêlée. Spirit, on the other hand, turns away from the fracas, and seeks the calm peace, love, and joy that acceptance ushers in. Where fear takes root, peace and joy never abide.

Courage Is Facing Fear

Courage is the quality resident in each person that recognizes fear for what it is and releases it appropriately. Courage is the ability to act, to take the next step, despite or in spite of the emotion that may dominate the body. Courage is not the absence of fear; rather, it is the quality that allows us to act while the energy of fear is present. Courage is the attribute of release. It takes courage to let go, to move out into the stream, to take the next small step forward into the great unknown.

Much of what we call evil is due entirely
to how we take the phenomenon.
Its sting can so often depart when,
after vainly seeking to shun it,
we agree to face about and bear it…

- William James -

Courage is the ability to let go despite all the evidence, made manifest by the ego, demanding you cling tightly to your present circumstances and limited ideas about reality.

The challenge, when the emotion of fear takes hold, has been labeled the "flight or fight syndrome." A person has three options: distance him- or herself from the threat (run away); resist the object of the threat (fight); or do nothing. The options to deal with the fear first require a response to the emotion and second an action to address the circumstances. The ego succeeds when we fall victim to emotion, fleeing, fighting, or succumbing to fear's paralysis. There is another way. That other way is to never become a channel for fear.

If you will now bear with me — here I digress, venturing into the realm of an ideal I have not realized. I have not yet brought this vista into view. For me, this possibility lies over the horizon. However, by continuing to seek the light, the promise and potential of overcoming fear draws closer...

Wisdom is the word used to describe the path to enlightenment, the road to enduring security. Through wisdom we recognize initially the nature of fear, and through wisdom aided by faith we finally come to exist in a state where we banish fear from our awareness. We overcome fear by dismissing its existence.

Life presents us a profound opportunity with regard to fear, the opportunity to eliminate the negative energy of fear by choosing a life of faith and positive expectation. To achieve this requires a spiritual connection to the source and the realization that we are visitors in a strange and marvelous land. As visitors we embrace this reality for the experiences it provides but never forget we are only on tourist visas. We enjoy our temporary stay, accept the passing of time, circumstances, possessions, and possibilities. Reveling in the moment, we are secure in the knowledge that no matter what this life brings — this reality of flesh and bones, air, earth, water and fire — it is temporary and transient. We, the awareness, the

By observing fear,
By exposing it to the light,
We reveal the deceit,
And in so doing,
Usher in the delight of possibility.

observer, are permanent and enduring. We, in essence belong to, are one with, a higher realm.

We truly are on the rollercoaster of life. Sometimes life moves fast, sometime life moves slow, but always it moves. We experience highs and lows, ups and downs. Emotion washes over us like waves crashing on the seashore. Circumstances come into our lives and situations change. This entire existence is punctuated by, or more accurately is — in motion. Life, this world, this existence is change. By recognizing we are the observer, we are awareness: we can act courageously to dissolve or overcome fear.

We are so close to this reality that our experience is we are one with it. We flow in a dynamic state, in constant motion. Recognizing this is from the seed of wisdom. Choosing to control the ride is from the seed of courage.

Circumstances and situations come to us either through the momentum of the collective or by way of our individual summoning. We have more control over our lives than many might believe. To exert control over the circumstances and quality of this existence requires both motivation and belief, desire and expectation. To manifest what we desire requires we choose, then, framed in the circumstance of motion, we must act. Asking, requesting, intending, desiring some end means control over the circumstances of life if you first have the ability to let go and second possess the courage to act.

The all-too-common alternatives to having the courage to take responsibility for life and to act are rather to react, wait, or, worse yet, hide from the attempt. By clinging to what is, or by clinging to what was, we eliminate the possibility. We stifle the courage and miss the opportunity to journey forward.

Courage is not the absence of fear but rather the willingness to move forward despite the risk. Propelled by desire, courage permits action to move forward. Simultaneously courage allows the actor to release the ties that bind, to let go, allowing positive momentum in life.

What the small man seeks in others,
The superior man seeks in himself.

- CONFUCIUS -

Seek to Find

A journey of a thousand miles begins with you...

We are spiritual beings vested in bodies, experiencing perspectives of this reality, taking it all in. We have tools available to navigate the sea of change. And that is precisely what this life is, a sea of change.

All is in motion. Our progression through time and space is a journey. We travel to explore and experience, to give and to grow. We can choose to be passenger or driver, the journey begins and ends with that choice. A journey of a thousand miles begins with one small step; it begins with you.

We live literally and figuratively in the moment — NOW. There exists no other time. The past is memory; the future a dream. The moment is framed by the past and future; now is a bridge between the two. We never leave the bridge.

We can remember the past or, through a gift (some say a curse) of imagining, envision a future, but try as we might, we cannot escape the experience of now. This is a rule of the game. We are always at the synapse of energy in transition.

We are on a journey from here to there. This journey is the flow of energy through our perception. To change direction, seek.

Among the navigation tools available are: intellect (the radio tuner to ideas and memories), emotions, feelings, and the physical capacity to move through time and space, to change perspective. We are beings, each a localized essence of awareness, in a particular time and space experiencing this reality. At the same time we are, to a degree, swept up by the environment surrounding us.

The opportunity lies in employing our tools, setting our sails and navigating the sea of change to create the experience, the journey, the adventure we desire. Waiting until tomorrow only keeps us in port.

Courage is the capacity to confront what is imagined...

- LEO ROSTEN -

Act Despite Fear

We have devoted much time and attention to the concept and emotion of fear because fear is a primary tool of the ego. The primordial instinct that serves to keep us alive in a sometimes dangerous world has been corrupted by the ego and used against us, against the promise and potential of this life. Most are lost in the ego, in the power struggle of survival and control. The ego seeks to dominate. We, blind to the ego's intentions, seek comfort and solace in what we know. So enmeshed in the ego we learn to avoid fear rather than face it, and in so doing tie our own hands, bind our own thinking, limit our own possibilities. We must, to succeed in this life, come to terms with fear and through the seed of wisdom move beyond it.

The way to wisdom, the way to the secure knowledge that we are enduring, existing beyond our immediate circumstances, whole, safe and secure is by acting despite fear. Courage is the capacity to face fear, the ability to generate positive energy to overcome it. Fear is from the ego, and therefore is energy generated from within to paralyze us, keeping us from action.

Only by truly being at peace in this world will we eliminate fear from our experience. In the meantime, to move in the direction of promise and possibility we must act despite fear. We must face fear — not to combat it, but rather to recognize it when it exists.

We nurture fear with our intellects and our imaginations. In these circumstances, only by facing fear, only by stepping outside its influence through awareness, are we able to expose fear for the deception it is.

For those of us lost in the illusion — clinging tightly to the substance of this life — strength of desire is the lever to overcome fear. By recognizing, observing fear we dissolve it. Once we dissolve fear we can act. If we make a habit of acting despite fear, we come to a state of being where fear has no influence. Courage leads us to wisdom and wisdom to fulfillment.

Courage demands only
one small step —
the next step.

Take the Next Step

Life sometimes seems like a daunting challenge. The span, the tasks, the competition, the limitations all converge in the intellect to squelch motivation and restrict potential. When this happens and life seems overwhelming, recognize that we never take on the entire experience at once. We never reach the future — we only journey there in our minds. We live and play, laugh and cry, in the present. Our intentions bring to us the circumstances we find ourselves in. But we only leave "now" in our minds. We never face the entire spectrum of the future in its entirety, though we may perceive the prospect of the future in that way. Courage comes to our rescue. Through courage we move in the necessary direction, one small step at a time.

The events of life, the small slice of time, space and circumstances we mark as our existence are, by design, narrow. As human beings we have a limited natural capacity to adsorb and interpret. We can only experience so much. That capacity to experience, however, is much greater than most of us realize. The ego clouds our awareness with all types of unnecessary "self-imposed" restrictions. To move forward in a positive direction, and to keep life and the events of living in perspective, we need only to move one small step. Courage allows us to move forward to achieve the promise and potential that is our gift, our birthright, our offering. This life requires we take only one small step, the next step. Nothing beyond that matters.

Accept, Forgive, Let Go, Live

Recalling the story of Maximillian and the horror the innocent faced in the Nazi death camps, we might easily ask, why didn't he and the other prisoners resist? Why didn't they fight? Rather than struggle Maximillian's story ends with release. The release, as you recall, had two parts. First, Maximillian calmed

We have only one fear:
The *fear of* letting *go.*

Forgiveness is letting *go!*

his mind, settled his intellect, and forgave his captors. Then he lifted his arm, offered his life, and in so doing overcame his ego. Maximillian, like the author of the note asking forgiveness for those who inflicted suffering, recognized his own face, his own humanity, in the face of his captors. He let the transgressions go and in so doing freed himself.

The chronicle of every life ends with release. Death forces us to let go. A misfortune of life is clinging so tightly to the known. Whether good or bad, we miss the opportunity to soar, to experience untold joy, to fulfill our potential. We fear.

Wisdom leads us down a humble path; courage allows us to overcome the energy, the emotion, of fear. The process to fulfillment is the same: accept, forgive, let go, live. In the end the steps will be the same but through our resistance, through the power and influence of our ego, we may cram the process into the last gasp of breath as we close this chapter of existence and depart this life.

We will have no choice, in the end. Today, however, we have a choice. By letting transgressions go, by forgiving, we free ourselves. Courage allows us to break the ties of hate and discontent that we believe originate out there, but in fact bind our own hands, limit our own opportunity, and repress our own true spirit. Forgiveness is letting go. Forgiving takes courage.

Courage is the capacity to overcome the ego's resistance to the circumstances of life — the tendency to judge, the desire to control, and the need to cling to the known. Courage allows us to move beyond these self-imposed limitations and act in ways that usher in peace of mind, harmony of intent and joy of spirit.

When fear grips,
Observe its energy,
Release its hold,
Let go,
Move on.

Courage to go; to act; to let go

Maximillian found himself in arguably the worst circumstances possible: in a concentration camp where fear and hate reigned, and violence, murder, and death were the order of the day. Despite the depravity around him Maximillian maintained peace of heart, shared to the last, and offered his very life courageously, overcoming the bondage of fear. Maximillian embraced the opportunity to live, fully, joyfully, fearlessly to the very end. Maximillian overcame fear.

Fear is a natural formation of energy designed to ensure we survive in physical existence. Most often, however, in this modern life, fear is corrupted and employed by the ego to limit experience. Fear is from the ego. Until we embrace wisdom and embody faith to eliminate fear from our being, the only way to free ourselves from fear's influence is to face it. We must recognize the energy of fear, bring ourselves into the moment, and expose fear to the light of awareness. By observing fear, we reduce its influence and empower ourselves to act despite negative emotion. By facing fear, we overcome it.

Courage is the capacity to act despite fear. We need not shoot for the stars, swing for the fence, or attempt to do it all. Courage demands we only do what is necessary, that is, take the next small step. Intellectually we tend to look at life as a linear progression, a journey from here to there. Using this construct — until we realize life is full, whole and complete, all the time, all around us — we need only prepare for and act to invite in the next experience. Take the next step.

Life is a contact sport. Courage allows us to make contact, one step at a time.

The key to achieving the goal of living an inspired and joyful life is the process wisdom embraces and courage allows:

Accept, Forgive, Let Go, Live.

Pray for wisdom.
If you are wise, your life will be full.

If you cannot grasp wisdom,
Pray for courage.
Courage to let go leads to wisdom . . .

Strength

to Act
to Overcome

In weakness power reaches perfection.

- 2 Corinthians 12:9 -

Ed and Blanche were honest, hardworking people, but very poor. Ed worked as a railroad porter and handyman. Blanche cooked, cleaned, and did laundry for wealthy white families in north central Tennessee.

In 1940, millions of Americans were poor, out of work and homeless because of the Great Depression. Times were hard for everyone so there was no sense wallowing in self pity. Plenty of work needed to be done. Though Ed and Blanche didn't have much, somehow they always had enough.

Ed and Blanche lived lives of commitment and optimism. Not boasting many possessions, they had treasure in the children they nurtured and raised together. They managed to make ends meet by utilizing every scrap they could find for their large and growing family. Blanche went so far as to make dresses for the girls out of flour sacks.

Ed and Blanche had 19 children and another on the way, a shining star to add to their collection. Of all the members of Ed and Blanche's family, this new star had the biggest obstacles to overcome but was destined to shine the brightest.

Having few funds and many mouths to feed, healthcare was a luxury Ed and Blanche could ill afford. But Wilma, loath to wait, decided to join the family at her good time. Wilma was born prematurely, on June 23. She weighed in at a scant four and a half pounds. Because of racial segregation, Wilma and her mother were not permitted to be cared for at the local hospital in Clarksville. It was for whites only.

Wilma's life proved a challenge from the outset. With only one black doctor in Clarksville, and such a tight budget, Blanche committed the next several years to nursing Wilma through one illness after another. Ultimately, Blanche's sacrifice and Wilma's achievements grew to be testaments to the strength of the human character.

Wilma, an underdog from the very beginning, spent the bulk of her childhood in bed. Early on, she suffered from double pneumonia, and if that wasn't enough to test her young body, scarlet fever struck next. To round out her potpourri of illnesses, Wilma endured measles, mumps, and chicken pox. She experienced, or rather, endured, a full helping of childhood diseases. Though Wilma did not always fare well in her battles with disease, Ed and Blanche were always confident Wilma would survive, and survive she did.

The family put stock in the adage that what doesn't kill you makes you stronger. Wilma had more than her fair share of strength-building experiences.

Though home health care was the norm at the time, Wilma, at age four, had to be taken to the doctor when Blanche realized Wilma's left leg and foot were becoming weak and deformed. Blanche was told Wilma suffered from polio, a crippling disease that had no cure. The doctor told Blanche that Wilma would never walk. But Blanche would not give up on Wilma. As Wilma later in life recalled, "My doctors told me I would never walk again. My mother told me I would. I believed my mother."

Blanche, always wanting the best for her children, found out that Wilma could be treated at Meharry Hospital, the black medical college of Fisk University in Nashville. Even though it was 50 miles away, Wilma's mother took her there twice a week for two years, until she was able to walk with the aid of a metal leg brace. Then the doctors taught Blanche how to do physical therapy exercises at home. All of Wilma's brothers and sisters helped, too. The whole family did everything they could to encourage Wilma to be strong and work hard at getting well.

Around the house there were always plenty of brothers and sisters to serve as "lookouts" if Wilma mischievously removed her braces. "I spent most of my time trying to figure out how to get them off," Wilma reminisced. "When you come from a large, wonderful family, there's always a way to achieve your goals."

Years of treatment and a determination to be a "normal kid" worked. Through daily leg massages administered in turn by different members of her family, Wilma progressed to the point where she was able to abandon her leg braces and walk only with the aid of a special shoe.

During those years of physical therapy, Wilma was tutored at home by her mom and siblings. Her crippled leg made it impossible to attend school. When she could walk well enough, she faced the disadvantage of attending a poorly funded, inadequately equipped, segregated school. To young Wilma, who had known nothing but struggle all her brief life, being able to be with her brothers and sisters at a real school was a blessing, regardless of the conditions.

Blanche taught Wilma very early to believe she could achieve any goal she set. The first was to walk without braces; the next was to get out of that shoe.

Wilma's brothers erected a basketball goal in their backyard. Blanche recalled, "After that, it was basketball, basketball, basketball." Wilma had had enough of sitting on the sidelines. Wilma wasn't very good at first. She wasn't very strong and she wasn't very fast, but the same determination that had shed that brace changed all that.

Wilma ran with her brothers and sisters and their friends around the school playground and around their backyard. When the children would race Wilma would always come in last. But losing did not discourage her. Wilma knew that if she worked at it she would get stronger and faster.

Wilma ran and ran and ran every day, acquiring a sense of determination, a sense of spirit to never, never give up, no matter what else happened. By the time she was 12 she was challenging every boy in her neighborhood at running, jumping, everything. She worked so hard she gained the strength to walk normally, without crutches, a brace, or a corrective shoe. Wilma overcame her weakness. By the time she was 13, she was outrunning her neighborhood friends in informal races and beating stiff competition in pick-up basketball games.

Having achieved her goal — to discard the shoe — she set her sights on becoming an athlete.

In junior high, Wilma followed her older sister Yolanda's example and joined the basketball team. The coach didn't put Wilma in a single game for three years. But quitting was not in her nature. Wilma continued to practice and improve her skills. Determination and heart were among Wilma's defining qualities.

Finally, in her sophomore year at Burt High School in Clarksville, Wilma became the starting guard. She excelled in her new role and soon became a star. Wilma set new Tennessee high school basketball scoring records, once scoring 49 points in a single game. As an all-state player Wilma led her team to a state championship.

During the state basketball tournament, Wilma was spotted by Ed Temple, the coach for the famous Tigerbelles, the women's track team at Tennessee State University. Because Burt High School didn't have the funding for a track team, coach Temple invited Wilma to Tennessee State for a summer sports camp.

Wilma had natural ability she couldn't explain. "I don't know why I run so fast," she said. "I just run."

Wilma loved sprinting enough to begin attending Temple's daily college practices while still in high school. Temple's dedication was inspiring. He was a sociology professor at Tennessee State and an unpaid coach. He drove the team to meets in his own car and had the school track, an unmarked and unsurfaced dirt oval, lined at his own expense.

But Temple was no soft touch. He made the girls run an extra lap for every minute they were late to practice. Wilma once overslept practice by 30 minutes and was made to run 30 extra laps. The next day she was sitting on the track 30 minutes early.

Unity and teamwork were Temple's passions. His passion proved to be life lessons for young Wilma.

Wilma excelled at track. She was undefeated as a sprinter in all of her high school track meets. In 1956, at the tender age of 16, Wilma went to her first Olympic Games in Melbourne, Australia, winning a bronze medal in the 4 by 400-meter relay.

Upon graduating from high school in 1957, Wilma received a full scholarship to Tennessee State University. She began setting her sights on the next Olympic Games. In the interim, she gained national recognition in collegiate meets, setting the world record for 200 meters.

At the 1960 Olympics in Rome, Wilma earned the title of the "World's Fastest Woman," winning three gold medals. In the 100 meters, she tied the world record of 11.3 seconds in the semifinals, then won the final by three yards in 11.0. Because of a 2.75-meter per second wind — above the acceptable limit of two meters per second — she didn't receive credit for a world record. In the 200, she broke the Olympic record in the opening heat in 23.2 seconds and won the final in 24.0 seconds. Wilma and her whole team were elated, but she had more work to do.

Working toward the 400-meter relay final Wilma sprained her ankle. No stranger to adversity, she ignored the pain to help her team. In the semifinals Wilma's team, all women from Tennessee State, set a world record of 44.4 seconds. In the finals, despite a poor baton pass, Wilma overtook Germany's anchor leg, earning the Americans the gold in 44.5 seconds.

These record-setting achievements led Wilma to become one of the most celebrated female athletes of all time. Always gracious, Wilma didn't forget her teammates; she said her favorite event was the relay because she got to stand on the platform with them.

The press and fans flocked to see Wilma in Rome. After the Olympics, when the team competed in Greece, England, Holland, and Germany, it was the charming, beautiful Wilma, fans wanted to watch perform. The first American woman to win three Olympic golds, she was named the Associated Press and United Press U.S. Female Athlete of the Year for 1960.

Wilma's celebrity broke gender and racial barriers. There was one "first" accomplishment that was more special than any of the others. Wilma insisted that her homecoming parade in Clarksville, to celebrate her Olympic triumph, be open to everyone and not a segregated event, as was the usual custom. Her victory parade was the first racially integrated event ever held in the town. The banquet the townspeople held that night, in her honor, was the first time in Clarksville's history that blacks and whites had ever gathered together for the same event.

Wilma recognized the injustice of segregation laws and went on to participate in protests in Clarksville until the segregation laws were struck down.

Because of her celebrity, Wilma took time off from her studies to make appearances and compete in international track events. She did more than promote her country. In her soft-spoken, gracious manner, she paved the way for African-American athletes, both men and women, who came later.

Realizing the importance of education Wilma returned to Tennessee State. She earned a Bachelor's Degree in education, graduating in 1963. The same year, Wilma married her high school sweetheart, Robert Eldridge. They had four children together: Yolanda, Djuanna, Robert Jr., and Xurry.

In 1963, Wilma was selected to represent the U. S. State Department as a Goodwill Ambassador at the Games of Friendship in Dakar, Senegal. Later that year she was invited by Dr. Billy Graham to join the Baptist Christian Athletes in Japan.

After retiring from track competition, Wilma returned to Clarksville to live. She taught at her old school, Cobb Elementary, and was the track coach at her alma mater, Burt High School. She replaced her old coach, who, tragically, had been killed in an auto accident.

Wilma was showered with honors the rest of her life. Despite her athletic prowess Wilma thought God had a greater purpose for her. In 1967, Vice President Hubert Humphrey invited Wilma to participate in "Operation Champ," an athletic outreach program for underprivileged youth in the ghettoes of 16 major cities. She started what she labeled her greatest accomplishment, her own non-profit organization. Wilma wanted to help children learn about discipline, hard work, and how to face and overcome adversity, as she had her whole life. "I tell them that the most important aspect is to be yourself and have confidence in yourself," Wilma said. "I remind them the triumph can't be had without the struggle." The foundation provided free coaching in a variety of sports, and academic assistance and support as well.

Small-town life proved to be too limiting for Wilma after all her worldly experiences. Her personal life was not without hardship. She eventually divorced and moved out on her own — a single mom — facing new challenges seeking new strength. She moved on to coaching positions, first in Maine, and then with DePauw University in Indiana.

Wilma continued to touch Olympians and non-Olympians alike. She was invited to be the guest speaker at dozens of schools and universities. She also went into broadcasting and became a sports commentator on national television and the co-host of a network radio show. She published her autobiography, *Wilma*. Her story of adversity and triumph was made into a movie.

Wilma's enduring message was to, "Never underestimate the power of dreams and the influence of the human spirit. We are all the same in this notion. The potential for greatness lives within each of us."

Wilma understood that, "The triumph can't be had without the struggle. And I know what struggle is." She had one last test to face. She was still active and vibrant when diagnosed with brain cancer in her early 50s. She faced this disease as she had every other challenge in her life— with extraordinary calm and grace, humility and determination.

Wilma believed that, "When the sun is shining I can do anything; no mountain is too high, no trouble too difficult." She realized, however, this was to be her last strength-building exercise — her call home.

Wilma Rudolph died in her own bed, with her family at her side, in Nashville, Tennessee, on November 12, 1994. She was 54 years young. She was laid to rest with an Olympic flag over her coffin.[4]

Wilma's life is a story of achieving against the odds. Her first accomplishments were to stay alive and get well; then to grow strong and walk.

The crippled girl, who doctors once said would never walk, was a sight to behold. At 5-foot-11 and 130 pounds, she was lightning fast. Wilma watchers in the late '50s and early '60s were admonished: "Don't blink— you might miss her." And that would have been a shame.

Wilma faced challenges of disease, poverty, and discrimination. Overcoming adversity, she excelled to become the best in the world. At every turn she faced insurmountable obstacles, but at every turn she also found someone reaching out to her, pushing, pulling, or cajoling her forward. The strength she needed to survive, compete, triumph, and share was always at hand. Her faith and the faith of those who loved her and believed in her called the strength forth. Wilma spent a lifetime sharing what it meant to be strong so that others might have the chance to reach their dreams.

Contrast

A necessary component of what defines this existence, what characterizes the world we live in, the universe we see and sense, is contrast. We live in a dualistic reality, a reality of distinctions, observable differences, unique signatures, shades of grey — contrast. In a dualistic world we cannot have one side without the other; all events, all circumstances, all happenings, or, as Eckhart Tolle says, "all forms," come into awareness as packaged deals. Contrast is necessary to distinguish any "this" from "that," any single thing from all things.

We distinguish differences, make distinctions, recognize contrasts, as contrast is required for us to see. However, by our nature we often tend to amplify contrast and highlight differences as opposed to seeking similarities. Through the workings

The triumph can't be had without the struggle.

- Wilma Rudolph -

of ego, we separate what are interconnected, codependent pieces into isolated, independent parts. Through ego we create greater disparity, we sharpen contrast. Dualism is the element of this reality that makes experience fulfilling, rewarding and exciting, or painful, depressing, and tiresome. Without the contrast of dualism, all of what is, all that we recognize, would blend together. With contrast, we have life, we have this world, we have what we know.

Conflict

Sir Isaac Newton's third law of motion states that every action has an equal and opposite reaction, and every force has an opposing force. Newton, through his energy expression, highlights the duality of the natural world, the reality of opposites. Polar opposites are in fact extreme contrasts, conditions that cannot exist without each other. Conflict, in turn, is the action of opposing forces, competing energy. Conflict is the motion of contrast where apparently disconnected pieces or forces work toward what appear to be opposing, non-harmonious ends.

This reality presents nearly infinite possibilities, multiple perspectives with every circumstance. The potential for harmony or discord manifest in every situation. Opportunity is inherent in every crisis just as tragedy lurks in the shadow of triumph. Conflict appears as disparate interests, divergent forces, or contrasting intent. The friction of conflict is the natural law of resistance that, as strange as it seems, holds everything together; in a dualistic reality, one cannot separate opposites.

Like contrast, conflict is a necessary ingredient of this experience. Conflict need not be negative. Good things can and do come from conflict. The friction of divergent forces, contrary interests, is a means of summoning energy and broadening perspective, a means to gaining strength.

Problems are power in disguise.

Polar opposites come as packaged deals. The potential for harmony exists with the potential for discord. Though both potentials exist, our orientation and judgment will not necessarily bring both to light. Either we see the circumstances come together well, the parts converge and the system function harmoniously or we perceive only a part of the whole and discord reigns.

We differentiate among various possibilities in every circumstance, one from the other. We cause circumstances to be or influence outcomes by our attitude and orientation. We may either sharpen or reinforce contrast and conflict or soften dividing lines that merge opposing forces. We can, in fact, nurture harmony, ultimately achieving unity of intent and purpose and action. Nurturing harmony naturally recognizes we all (all people, all things) are in this together; we are one.

Strength

We define strength as power, force, might, vigor, potency, and so on, meaning the capacity to withstand adversity and to influence or control circumstances. Most often, strength is associated with "physical" ability; however, strength of character and strength of will have more far-reaching consequences.

We rely on a basic level of strength to exist in this reality. Nature places necessary pressure on our bodies while the complex of events and relationships stresses intellect. From a physical perspective, to be alive requires a minimum endowment of strength. Contrast and conflict are the nature of this reality, a nature we encourage every time we play a game. Games, whether athletic or intellectual are artificial circumstances we create to engage the properties of contrast and conflict to have fun. To survive in the environment of this reality requires the capacity to contribute to the dynamic tension, to generate and

Obstacles are tools for growth.

resist opposing forces. To stand we must resist the pull of gravity. To move we must overcome the inertia of a body at rest. Living requires strength.

Beyond the strength required to live, move, and grow, we humans have and further seek the ability to influence the environment and the circumstances of our existence. We desire strength of body, of mind, of will. We employ the strength we have to manipulate reality to conform to our desires. Frequently (or mostly) this occurs when ego hijacks our being. Ego seeks to exert itself by resisting the master plan, circumstances as they are, and the direction life is flowing. Instead of working harmoniously with life, ego seeks to stand at odds, oppose what is, and force the world to conform to its desires.

Seemingly we find ourselves in need of strength, beyond the strength of being in this physical reality, in a few, well-defined circumstances:

First, strength is the remedy for exhaustion. When the body, the mind, or the spirit grow weary strength revitalizes.

Second, strength is the ingredient required to take up a challenge. A challenge, by definition, is something beyond normal, sustained capacity to manage.

Third, strength is required to face an obstacle. When adversity rises into awareness — that is, when a hardship beyond mere inconvenience or nuisance stands to challenge intentions, direction, or quite possibly existence— strength is required.

Strength is that reserve of energy to apply to the task, the challenge at hand. Energy empowers the will, the intellect, and the body to exert influence, to progress, to move forward. Strength allows the individual to manipulate this reality and develop and maintain momentum to navigate.

Strength is the energy of contrast, the energy of conflict, the energy of intent, the energy of space and motion in a material

Build me a son whose wishbone will not be where his backbone should be; a son who will know Thee — and that to know himself is the foundation stone of knowledge.
Lead him, I pray, not in the path of ease and comfort, but under the stress and spur of difficulties and challenge. Here, let him learn to stand up in the storm; here, let him learn compassion for those who fall.

- General Douglas A. MacArthur -

world. We associate strength with resistance and with struggle. Strength is the energy, the capacity that allows the individual to carry on, to venture forth, to ascend with excitement or survive the descent.

The strength of victory is often the strength of submission, not so much to the outside world but to demons within (read "ego"). Rarely do we understand the power available to us. However, the source of strength, the font of power is always there, ready to supply the energy — physical, emotional, intellectual — needed to overcome.

Approaching Adversity

We have come to believe by social conditioning, observation of and functioning in the physical world under the influence of the ego, that life is a struggle, life is suffering. We recognize contrast and conflict characterize this existence; however, we have come to believe we exist in a finite world with limited resources. We are weighed down by the gravity (pun intended) of it all. We need to compete to survive and struggle to achieve. From the ego viewpoint we have been thrust onto a battlefield. We are left to fight to overcome obstacles and challenged to face adversity with grit and determination. That's just the way it is. But that's not the way it has to be.

This view of life as a struggle for survival, life as suffering indicates that we are lost in ego. We have come to believe we are separate, cut off from the source, alone in a bewildering, dangerous world. The only assets we have to engage the forces arrayed against us are our cunning and our strength. We can run, but we cannot hide. Our only recourse is to conserve our strength, apply our wit, and hope to come out on top, — somehow, some way, some time. All in all, pretty dim prospects.

All strength is from one source,
All power comes from, is of,
God;
We come from, are of,
God.

In the state of mind just described, adversity looms as an obstacle to face and fight. Strength is the capacity to wage the good fight, to struggle against the odds, to withstand the adversity. Lost in ego, our only hope is that we can continue to renew the strength needed to persevere. Those on this path, those resisting life's circumstances, standing and fighting, must seek out a wellspring of strength to carry on. There is another way.

All our strength — physical, emotional, intellectual — is from one source. And that source is not out there, it is within. Personal energy — strength — is renewed from the source. No matter how great the obstacle, how threatening the adversary, how bewildering the circumstance, or how exhausting the challenge, an unlimited supply of strength and determination is close at hand.

Like the butterfly that must struggle to emerge from its cocoon, without the struggle its wings would never become strong enough to fly. So, too must we face adversity — resistance — it's the nature of this world. How we approach the adversity and deal with the resistance makes all the difference in the quality of the experience.

Adversity helps us grow. Accompanying every event or circumstance is an opportunity for growth. The opportunity is always on the other side of the ego. We can and often do decide to tackle obstacles through the ego and in so doing engage in monumental struggles. Recognize that this is a choice. We can choose the challenge and find comfort in the struggle, joy in the attempt — success or failure. As President Theodore Roosevelt eloquently expressed it, "The credit goes to the one in the arena marred with sweat and blood, who strives valiantly, who dares greatly, who risks all in seeking great triumphs, for even if he fails he is not to be counted among those who know neither victory nor defeat."

Obstacles will look large or small to you according to whether you are large or small.

- Orison Swett Marden -

The energy, the strength, to experience and face the challenges of life is available in plenty if our orientation is not to stagnate but rather to move forward. Life is movement; we call on the energy in motion when we move in harmony with it. Strength will always come to aid in measure equal to need (it's a law of life).

However, struggle and strife need not be the way. We can choose again. We can choose a path of less resistance, less struggle, and greater harmony. By accepting "what is," we empower our awareness to summon into being a new reality, new circumstances. We seize the advantage when we go with the flow.

If, on the other hand, we are more inclined to resist, we become mired where we are. Life will make us feel weak, wear us down, leave us with no energy. The distance from exhaustion to exhilaration is the reach of one's attitude. Linking a negative attitude with a state of resistance is a recipe for disaster, a state of weakness. If that is the circumstance we choose to experience — relent and accept — we succeed. An alternative choice to weakness and despair is to summon strength. We always have strength at hand when we are in a state of openness and positive expectancy. We require strength only when we resist or bring circumstances into our awareness that seem bigger than we are.

Knowing we have an unlimited supply of strength available to us, and that no matter what obstacle we face the strength at hand grows correspondingly, we have two choices: to rely on the wellspring of strength to face each obstacle as a singular event (as British Prime Minister Winston Churchill said of life, "It's one damn thing after another.") or accept, submit, and thereby empower, choosing another way.

Before moving to that "other way," before discussing the alternative, let's review: The nature of this world is contrast

Strength is power:
To manifest,
Create,
Triumph over ego.

and conflict; challenge and resistance are necessary parts of the design. Adversity is required for the adventure. Strength is energy to survive and thrive in this world — physically, emotionally, intellectually. Strength is the energy to apply to our intentions. All strength originates from one source and that wellspring, that font of strength, is available to us without effort at all times in proportion to our need.

We never encounter an obstacle we do not have the capacity to face; unlimited strength creates, generates, and drives change. We are more capable than we think. We have access to unlimited power and unlimited ability — not always necessarily in the way we anticipate, desire, or prefer, but always through some means, some opportunity, some alternative.

A law of human existence is: "We always have strength enough."

Belief Brings Possibility

For some people, everything seems to come easily. Attitudes are positive, relationships reinforcing — whatever these people touch turns to gold and trappings of success abound. Even the challenges that inevitably arise, when faced by these people, seem more manageable. They navigate rough waters with ease. From the observer's perspective these people are "lucky." Taking liberty with an old adage, "Luck is not so much chance as it is opportunity meeting preparation," let's explore the luck of these blessed few.

We have considered a few times the idea of "humans as creators of life experience." That is, through some mysterious process human beings bring the physical environment, circumstances, and players into awareness to act out a drama and fulfill an aim. Through these creative contributions the individual completes the whole and serves a greater purpose.

The measure of your strength
is proportional to
the measure of your faith.

The individual provides his or her contribution through intent, in the form of expectations, desires, and focus.

"Lucky" people are able, somehow, to maintain a perspective, an attitude, different than the average person, regarding the events, the happenings, the circumstances of life. The "lucky" are able to generate and sustain the momentum of positive expectancy. They converge effortlessly with the positive forces of this reality. They invite in and create positive outcomes. Strength for "lucky" is positive expectation coupled with free spirit; they lack the resistance that plagues the rest of us. They recognize (even if unconsciously) they are tourists in an exotic land and they are not always in control, but that's okay. They accept. Along for the ride, they expect good things to happen and find joy in the experience.

Results are the consequence of expectation. The wealthy expect prosperity; they are open to it, so prosperity is their experience. Search as we might for tangible "cause and effect," in truth what expresses in this reality emerges from intentions beyond this time and space. What manifests for each individual is a product of expectation made possible by openness.

Luck — the notion of blind chance — is not a factor in life. What happens is by design and intent. We individuals, are the artisans, the craftsmen, the designers, the creators of experience. The experiences we come to label good and bad.

Belief is the individual's mental narrative that gives him or her an orientation toward the circumstances of life. Belief is the conviction that causes the individual to celebrate or curse the sunshine or the rain. Belief is the individual's sense of assurance that life is an opportunity, an adventure, or a sentence marked by trials and tribulation. The "lucky" live believing life is an adventure.

The example of wealth I offer is not meant to equate accumulation of things with happiness or success. Rather, wealth,

Fear not, for I am with you;
Be not dismayed, for I am your God.
I will strengthen you,
Yes, I will help you,
I will uphold you with my righteous hand.

- ISAIAH 41:101 -

as used here, is an easily understood illustration (and often-misdirected goal), readily identified with by ego, of contrasting results in life. So it is with strength and weakness: by deliberate attitudes and actions (even an unconscious orientation), by being open to the source, we always get what we need.

The rich expect and are open to wealth manifesting in their experience. They let go, stop resisting, and their expectations are fulfilled. The same process occurs with any challenge, obstacle, or desire in life. When we truly fix intention to take up a challenge, face an obstacle, or set our sights on some achievement; when we open ourselves, strength fills us.

Strength is energy to overcome, energy to address challenges, energy to continue to move, energy to invoke or react to change. Strength is the character of the will to not succumb to doubt, not give in to despair, not yield to circumstances, but rather to continue to forge ahead despite the opposition, despite the adversity, despite the odds.

We have access to an unlimited supply of energy needed to move forward, to take the next step. If we are open the strength we need is always there. Ultimately, if we are open (if we let go, release resistance), anything is possible.

Consider a conceptual formula for manifesting to create anything and everything in this reality. Positive expectation minus resistance equals positive result. Expressed another way, optimistic desire plus openness manifests affirming experience. On the contrary, negative expectation manifests negative experience — resistance results in stagnation. Resistance causes us to languish. The tighter we cling, the less life moves. Life brings us what we expect or what we cling to.

Do you sense something missing in the expression? Another reinforcing element is at play in our equation. That component, not defined, is the orientation of the nature of this reality — the master plan, the drama's script. Ultimately, are the invisible

Positive Expectation – Resistance =
Positive Result

Or

Positive Desire + Openness =
Positive Result

forces of the universe for us? Against us? Or unbiased, indifferent toward our existence?

I offer this: first, the master plan intends that life be an opportunity, an adventurous dream. Second, regardless of the gravity of the master plan, what we "believe" determines our reality. What we believe about life colors our experience and influences us to judge good or bad — and so it is.

Means to Overcome

Challenges help us stretch and learn and grow. The strength we need is always available to overcome any and every obstacle we encounter, create, or believe is in our path. If God is for us, who can be against us?

Buried in every crisis is opportunity. Every force is counterbalanced. Every challenge, large or small, has a means to overcome evident in it (or sometimes not so evident — but there still, nonetheless). Measuring up to a challenge, calling for, and employing energy to achieve a desire or overcome an obstacle is a means to growth. The only requirement to succeed, to change circumstances, is a willingness to move on.

Despite our access to a reserve of strength, most often we fall victim to a desire to cling (ego) to current circumstances. When this happens, what we take on, what we resist, is the very force of change; we resist life itself. We challenge the nature of reality, fixing ourselves in time and space to dance the last dance, to act out the drama again and again, to fight the good fight.

The strength to overcome is accessible; all we need to do is couple the energy with a willingness to move on. The means to overcome is always present. The energy, the strength, is available to the extent of our individual capacity to change, to journey on, to grow.

Life intends to grow.
You can intend to go along,
Or resist.
Use your strength wisely.

Let Go, Stop Resisting

Strength is the energy to drive change, but it is also the energy to endure until new circumstances develop, apparently unaided by our hand. Another way exists — a path of least resistance. By this path obstacles are dissolved, challenges reduced, adversaries eliminated. By this least traveled path we come to manifest a reality in harmony with and supporting the whole. We come to an enduring state of peace and joy.

You've read these words many times, if you have lasted this long — "Life is an opportunity," "Life is an adventure." The measure of life we each possess is an opportunity of promise and potential. This reality is so consuming that we are in the drama and are the drama. We are so caught up being actors we forget we are directors — creators and observers.

Everything we have and do, accept and reject, nurture and destroy, affects and contributes to the whole. In contrast, everything — the world, the universe, the people, the environment, the events, the circumstances — are all for us: for you individually, for your pleasure, your education, and your growth, whole and complete. Another paradox for the intellect, but a truth nonetheless: life is for, about, because of, the individual; life is for, about, because of, the whole.

We are here, in this reality, with a means, a capacity, to navigate — a capacity to move and a capacity to resist. We can linger or we can create and move on. We have the ability to choose to navigate or stand still, resist or cooperate, create or destroy. Strength enables these choices.

The purpose for our being may not be evident: it may not be plain, yet we are here, we are in the river, we are on the ride. We have command of a wellspring of power, we can use that energy, that strength, to resist or we can joyfully join the dance. Stop resisting — let go!

All things ARE possible...

Strength to act; to overcome

✦ Contrast and conflict are elements of this reality. ✦

✦ We never face an obstacle we do not have the means to overcome. ✦

✦ The approach to adversity makes all the difference. ✦

✦ All things are possible to one who believes. ✦

Living a life of and from the source, a life of wisdom, is the goal. If wisdom seems lofty and unattainable, if we've not embraced the promise and potential, courage allows us the opportunity to take the next step. Strength is the energy of that step.

"The story of me" seems one challenge, one obstacle after another. It seems the sole purpose of everything — people, objects, events — is to derail us, beat us down, make us submit. We grow weary and tire of the struggle. Yet, upon reflection, we realize we have managed to survive, to move past all the events of the drama called "my life" up until now. No matter what we faced, somehow, some way, things changed and we moved on. This too will pass.

We have found the enemy, and the enemy is us. Our attitudes toward the events of life, the happenings that flitter through our awareness, can overwhelm, if we resist and struggle. "Whose sins are loosed on earth are loosed in heaven; whose sins are bound on earth are bound in heaven…" (John 20:23) We bind ourselves.

However, the strength of the source is always available to us. We create, design, build, and maintain the world we live in, the reality we experience. Our attitudes and choices shape the circumstances we call into our awareness. Like Wilma Rudolph, we are vessels, entry points of energy into the master design. Strength flows to aid based on need. By ceasing to resist, we allow the flowering of promise and the fulfilling of potential.

Stop Resisting, Let Go — Let God!

Pray for wisdom.
If you are wise, your life will be full.

If you cannot grasp wisdom,
Pray for courage.
Courage to let go leads to wisdom.

If you cannot claim courage,
Pray for strength.
Strength to overcome leads to courage…

Will

to Choose
to Persevere

Yet not my will, but yours be done.
- LUKE 22:42 -

Set your sails — choose your life story.

"I do solemnly swear that I will faithfully execute the office of President of the United States, and will to the best of my ability, preserve, protect and defend the Constitution of the United States." These are words not lightly spoken nor easily arrived at. From humble beginnings to hallowed halls of power — what character, what circumstances, what choices make it possible for one capable, appealing, charming but still mere mortal to rise from obscurity to nobility over the course of a working lifetime? Is it privilege? Opportunity? Preparation? A combination of these? Or something else?

James Earl Carter Jr., was born October 1, 1924, in Plains, Georgia. Peanut farming, talk of politics, and devotion to the

Baptist faith were mainstays of his upbringing. Jimmy came from a family with deep roots in Georgia. His great grandfather served in the Confederate Army, seeing considerable action at the Battle of Gettysburg.

Jimmy, the first President born in a hospital, was the eldest of four children. Being the eldest brought with it certain responsibilities to honor. Life on a farm was full of hard work and shared challenges. Jimmy developed a fondness for reading at an early age and proved himself a gifted student. Besides academics, he excelled in sports, particularly basketball and football.

Opportunities seemed limited in a small southern farming community. But Jimmy was surrounded by people who saw otherwise. One of his most influential teachers was a woman by the name of Julia Coleman. Julia had suffered from polio, but through the power of her will had overcome great odds. Her encouragement and guidance profoundly influenced Jimmy's development.

Jimmy's discipline, organizational skills, and intellectual insight led him to Georgia Southwestern College and Georgia Institute of Technology. His academic success culminated in an invitation to attend the prestigious U.S. Naval Academy in Annapolis, Maryland. Jimmy was led to an environment that fit him like a glove. He excelled at the Academy, graduating in the top 10 percent of his class.

Following graduation from the Naval Academy in 1946, Jimmy made a key decision that shaped the rest of his life. He married Rosalynn Smith, a devoted and loving woman. The Carters had three sons, Jack, Chip, and Jeff, and a daughter, Amy. Family was always a top priority.

In the Navy Jimmy served on submarines. Continuing his commitment to excellence he proved himself a superior officer. He was selected by Captain (later Admiral) Hyman G. Rickover to become a leader of the fledgling nuclear submarine program.

Rickover was demanding but fair — expecting the best from the men he commanded — and Jimmy delivered.

Jimmy loved the Navy. He planned to make the Navy a career, and his goal was to become Chief of Naval Operations (the senior uniformed position in the Department of the Navy). But his path was not on the high seas. Jimmy's father died suddenly in July 1953. Lieutenant Carter immediately resigned his commission to take over the family peanut farming business in Plains.

Family, farming and faith were the devotions of energetic Jimmy, but he constantly looked for additional ways to assist his fellow man. He started his political career serving on various local boards. In 1962 he made a new career choice; he entered state politics and won a seat in the state Senate. Eight years later, after one failed attempt, he was elected Governor of Georgia. His careful planning and tireless dedication secured the victory.

Among new young Southern governors, Jimmy attracted attention by emphasizing ecology, efficiency in government, and the removal of racial barriers. Once again he proved himself capable and far-sighted. Running for President, however, was a whole other league. When Jimmy told his family he intended to run for President, his mother asked, "President of what?" But once again, through dogged determination, insightful strategizing, strong team building, and winning optimism Jimmy became President of the United States. He chose a challenging course.

After serving as President for four years Carter reflected on the job, "the Presidency is a place of compassion…

"The life of every human being on Earth can depend on the experience, judgment and vigilance of the person in the Oval Office. The President's power for building and his power for destruction are awesome...

"The President of the United States is the steward of the Nation's destiny. He must protect our children and the children they will have and the children of generations to follow. He must speak and act for them. That is his burden and his glory...

"The President is a servant of today, but his true constituency is the future."

Ronald Wilson Reagan was born on February 6, 1911, in the small town of Tampico, Illinois. His father was a tough Irish-American shoe salesman; his mother was of Scottish-Irish descent. Ronald preferred the nickname "Dutch" to his given name. His father had said that Ronald looked like a "fat little Dutchman" when he was born and the name stuck.

Throughout Dutch's early years, the Reagan family hopscotched across Illinois. They lived in Tampico, Chicago, Galesburg, and Monmouth; settling finally in Dixon when Dutch was nine. Because of the frequent moves, and his shy nature, Dutch didn't make many, if any, lasting friendships. Instead, he looked to his family for company, his parents and brother Neil. Together they forged a tight-knit unit.

The small, rural community of Dixon proved to be a great place for young boys to come of age. Everyone knew one another and helped each other in times of need. Dutch came out of his shell in Dixon, tromping many a day through the woods with friends, swimming and fishing in the local river, trapping muskrats, and getting into mischief.

Competing with the other boys caused Dutch to get in a number of fights, but he didn't want to be a ruffian. Instead, he became a fairly devout Christian. His mother, a Disciple of Christ, had never pressured her sons into becoming disciples themselves. Dutch decided on his own to be baptized. His faith strongly influenced the rest of his life.

Dutch's mom instilled a sense of decorum and an unconditional generosity in her boys. She firmly believed in helping those less fortunate and came to despise the adverse effects of alcohol. Ironically, Dutch's father was an alcoholic, his mother, though, accepted his weakness and made the best of her circumstances.

The Reagans were not a wealthy family. On the contrary, often they could barely make ends meet. Dutch's parents, lacking formal education, relied on what he later called "street smarts." They saw education as a way to prosperity and encouraged their sons to work hard in school.

By the time he went to high school, Dutch had decided sports were more enjoyable than academics. This did not square with his parent's intentions, so he never really let his studies go. Dutch took a particular liking to football. Though he didn't possess the physical skills of the best athletes he brought a relentless work ethic and positive attitude to the team.

He also found a new avocation — one far removed from the young introvert of his former life — acting. Dutch secured the lead in several church and school plays. Acting really brought Dutch out of his shell. He emerged as a talented, affable leader, becoming student body president his senior year.

After high school, opportunity beckoned. Dutch entered Disciples of Christ Eureka College, in Eureka, Illinois, in 1928. Dutch leveraged his skills and genial manner in college to become a popular student leader. And again, like in high school, he made time for academics, but concentrated on extracurricular activities — college politics and sports.

Majoring in economics and sociology, he continued to develop his acting talent. He recognized that effective communication skills were a key to success in any field. He chose wisely. Over the course of his college career he won several prestigious acting awards.

The spotlight of media appealed to the good-looking, gregarious, ambitious young man. Upon graduation Dutch became a radio sports announcer. He did not abandon his ambition, however, a screen test in 1937 won him a contract in Hollywood. He pursued his acting career as he did everything in life, with passion and optimism. Over the course of the next two decades he appeared in 53 films.

Dutch married an actress, Jane Wyman. Together they had two children. Unfortunately, as with many Hollywood marriages, theirs was not destined to last. They divorced in 1948. In 1952, Dutch married, "the love of his life," Nancy Davis, also an actress, and this union worked. In Nancy, Dutch found a devoted partner to share life's troubles and triumphs. Dutch had two more children with Nancy.

While working as an actor, Dutch promoted his political ambitions through practical means. He became the president of the Screen Actors Guild. Through this platform and while working as a television host he promoted conservative values and built his reputation until he was ready to throw his own hat in the ring and run for public office.

In 1966 Dutch was elected Governor of California, the nation's most populous state, by a margin of a million votes. He proved himself an adept administrator, talented communicator, and insightful politician. He won a second term as Governor in 1970, but he had grander ambitions. With Nancy serving as a sounding board and confidant, he chose differently. He passed on a run for a third term as California's governor, instead setting his sights on national office — nothing less than President.

With the Republican Party struggling to overcome a tarnished reputation, Dutch made a run for the Republican nomination against an incumbent President in 1976. He nearly succeeded in his bid, narrowly loosing the primary to President Gerald Ford. The setback did not dim Dutch's ambition. The nation was at a crossroads and Dutch was determined to steer a new course. Dutch, Ronald Wilson Reagan, won the Presidency with two-thirds of the popular vote in 1980, ushering in a new era of American optimism.

George Herbert Walker Bush was born on June 12, 1924 at 173 Adams Street in Milton, Massachusetts. This was an auspicious location, as Adams Street is named for the family of Presidents John Adams and John Quincy Adams, who lived on the same street just a few miles south in the neighboring community of Quincy. George was from a family of privilege, but his parents drove home the message that it is a privilege to serve your fellow man. So a lifetime of public service was what George chose.

Soon after George's birth the Bush family moved from Milton to Greenwich, Connecticut, where George began his formal education at the Greenwich Country Day School. Being from a family of means, George was able to attend the exclusive and prestigious Phillips Academy in Andover, Massachusetts. Always seeking responsibility, George secured numerous leadership positions at the academy.

By June 1942, the United States was building up its military might to strike against the Axis powers, having suffered the blow at Pearl Harbor the previous December. George chose to serve. After graduating from Phillips Academy, he joined the U.S. Navy on his eighteenth birthday, intending to fly. He completed the 10-month training course days before his nineteenth birthday. He was commissioned an ensign, the youngest naval aviator to that date.

Young George was immediately assigned to a torpedo squadron as a photographic officer. His squadron, based on the U.S.S. San Jacinto, participated in combat operations against Marcus and Wake Islands in May 1944. In June, he fought in one of the largest air battles of the war in the Marianas. Casualties were high on both sides. George had to put his emergency and survival training to use as his aircraft made a forced water landing. The young pilot and his crew survived. A destroyer came by and collected them.

George, promoted to Lieutenant Junior Grade, was soon embroiled in operations against the Japanese in the Bonin Islands. On September 2, 1944, George faced the biggest challenge of his wartime service. He piloted one plane of a four attack aircraft formation to strike the Japanese installations on Chichi Jima. Each crew consisted of a pilot, radioman, and gunner. Nearing the target, the attack flight endured intense antiaircraft fire. George's plane was hit, igniting the engine. Despite the burning engine, George pressed on to his target, releasing bombs to score several damaging hits. George struggled to maintain his plane aloft. Finally, in desperation, George called for his crew to abandon the craft. Only George and one crew member made it out. While George's chute deployed, the other man's parachute did not — he plummeted to his death. George received the Distinguished Flying Cross for his actions.

Despite being shot down, George continued to contribute to the naval offensive. Immediately after his rescue he worked for a month assisting in the rescue of other downed pilots. Subsequently he returned to the San Jacinto and participated in operations in the Philippines. When his ship finally returned to port in Guam, George's squadron, which had suffered 50 percent pilot casualties, was replaced and sent back to the States. In total, George flew 58 combat missions and was awarded the Distinguished Flying Cross, three Air Medals, and the Presidential Unit Citation. He had proved himself an American hero.

Back in the States, George found romance. He married a strong, capable woman, Barbara Pierce. Their union produced six children and paved the way for great accomplishments.

With the war still raging, George was assigned to Norfolk, Virginia, where he put his valuable combat experience to use training new torpedo pilots. After imparting his experience, it was time to go back in to action — a prospect Barbara did not find particularly appealing. He was reassigned as a torpedo pilot bound for the Pacific. With the Japanese surrender, however, he was not to see combat again. He was honorably discharged in September 1945 and, like so many World War II vets, he chose to pursue higher education. He entered Yale University.

Back at school, George continued to seek out leadership opportunities, in a fraternity and as a talented athlete. Knowingly he cultivated relationships with influential people at every turn; he moved in powerful circles.

After graduating from Yale in 1948, George went into the oil exploration business in Texas. After some success, his penchant for public service rose to the fore. With a host of influential connections and a reputation for excellence, George won the Republican Party's nomination for the U.S. Senate from Texas in 1964, but not the election. Undeterred, he was elected to the U.S. House of Representatives from the 7th District of Texas in 1966.

In 1970 George relinquished his House seat to again run for Senate at the urging of President Nixon. After losing the Senate race by a slim margin, George was appointed Ambassador to the United Nations by President Nixon. Thereafter George circulated in elite Washington power circles building a résumé that included stints as Chairman of the Republican National Committee, Chief of the U.S. Liaison Office in the People's Republic of China, and Director of Central Intelligence.

After a Democratic administration took power in 1977, George became Chairman of the First International Bank in Houston and Adjunct Professor of Administrative Science at Rice University. During his years back in Texas he built his organization for a presidential run in 1980. He distinguished himself as Vice President under Ronald Reagan. With a life dedicated to public service and an impressive résumé, George Herbert Walker Bush attained the nation's highest office in 1988.

William Jefferson Clinton spent the first six years of his life in Hope, Arkansas. His father, William Jefferson Blythe, was killed in an auto accident several months before his mother gave birth to the future President on August 19, 1946. Raised in his grandmother's home, Bill's early years were dominated by two strong-willed women who often competed for his attention. Bill found the relationship between his mother and grandmother to be challenging, as he was often cast as the young mediator.

In 1950, Bill's mother married Roger Clinton, a car dealer and abusive alcoholic. The family relocated to Hot Springs, Arkansas, a bustling resort town an hour from Bill's grandmother's house. With his mom in a tumultuous marriage, Bill found himself dealt the mediator role again.

Bill excelled in school and nurtured a passion for politics. Having developed an ear for gospel music, found through his Baptist faith, he took up the saxophone. He balanced the adventure of the local gambling dens and mineral spas with church and politics. Among the locals, he was widely recognized as a young man of rare talent and ambition.

The principal of Hot Springs High School was a powerful force in public education. She recruited staff committed to producing public service leaders. Bill became her brightest protégé. Through her efforts Bill landed a position as one of two Arkansas delegates to Boy's Nation, an imitation political convention sponsored by the American Legion, in Washington, D.C. At the conference Bill met President John F. Kennedy at the White House. Bill's mother had always told him he would be President some day. He left Boy's Nation determined to fulfill her prediction.

Upon graduation from high school in 1964, Bill left Arkansas bound for Georgetown University in Washington, D.C. Facing class barriers, Bill employed his energy, dashing good looks, and captivating charm to lead the student government and secure the presidency of his freshman and sophomore classes. Uncharacteristically, he was not elected his junior year. He looked too calculating and disingenuous to his peers, and he learned a lesson from the experience.

Beginning in his junior year, Bill worked as a clerk for the U.S. Senate Foreign Relations Committee. The people he worked for and around greatly shaped his perspective on the Vietnam War. He came to believe the U.S. had no moral or strategic reason for being in Vietnam. Just prior to his graduation from Georgetown, he won a prized Rhodes scholarship to study at Oxford University in England for two years. The prospect of being drafted for the war hung over head as he set sail for England.

While in England, Bill received his draft notice. He returned to Arkansas to work out his situation. He temporarily secured some relief from the draft and returned to Oxford. Finally, in the fall of 1969, after much maneuvering and personal moral conflict, he chose to subject himself to the draft. He lucked out, drawing a high number in the lottery, virtually assuring he would not be called. Bill capitalized on his time at Oxford, forging relationships with men and women who would later become part of his administration.

Following Oxford, Bill chose to enter Yale Law School. He earned his degree in 1973 and met his future bride, Hillary Rodham. While attending Yale his passion for politics led him to cut his teeth working on Senate (Joe Duffy in Connecticut) and Presidential (George McGovern) campaigns.

After graduating from law school, Bill moved back to Arkansas to teach law at the University of Arkansas in Fayetteville. Almost immediately upon arrival, he threw himself into politics, running for a seat in the U.S. House of Representatives. Though he lost this 1974 race, his strong showing proved him a rising star.

Two years later, Arkansas voters elected Bill state attorney general. Ever ambitious, in 1978, at age 32, Bill ran for governor. He won an easy victory to become one of the nation's youngest governors ever. However, his youth and inexperience quickly left Arkansans unimpressed. Consequently, the voters turned him out. He became the youngest former governor in American history.

Shocked by defeat, Bill went to work for a Little Rock law firm but spent most of his time campaigning for re-election. In the 1982 race, Bill admitted his mistakes and leveraged his charm to win another chance. He continued to serve as Arkansas's governor through three more terms.

Setting his sights higher, Bill cultivated a national profile, rising to chair the National Governors Association. He ran his governor's office like a continuous campaign and demonstrated the style and effectiveness of a progressive political leader. After overcoming serious impediments to achieving national public office, he secured the Presidency in 1992. He fulfilled his mother's prediction and his grandest lifelong ambition.

George Walker Bush, born July 6, 1946, in New Haven, Connecticut — often referred to as simply W — is the eldest son of former President George Herbert Walker Bush. W grew up in Midland, Texas, where his father worked in the oil business. He experienced early the frailty of life when his younger sister, Robin, died tragically of leukemia.

Like his father, W attended the prestigious Philips Academy in Andover, Massachusetts, then entered Yale University. He graduated from Yale with a Bachelor's degree in 1968. Returning to Texas, he joined the Texas Air National Guard. He learned to fly fighter jets, like his father. But unlike his father, he was never called on to fight.

The early 1970s were aimless years for W. He worked intermittently as a management trainee at an agricultural firm and on U.S. Senate campaigns in Florida and Alabama. W later admitted that the early 1970s were a nomadic period in his life marked by heavy drinking. He did succeed, however, at Harvard Business School, earning his M.B.A. in 1975.

Still following in his father's footsteps, W decided to try his hand at the oil business. He returned to Midland, Texas, and formed an independent oil and gas exploration company. He also had the good fortune of meeting and marrying a former teacher and librarian, Laura Welch. Laura gave birth to twin daughters, Barbara and Jenna, in 1981.

While developing his business ventures, W joined the 1978 race for the U.S. House of Representatives. He won a tough victory in the primary, and raised huge amounts of money for his campaign, but ended up losing the election. He did, however, sew the seeds for a new vocation.

In the early 1980s, W reorganized his oil business ventures and merged with an oil-investing fund. He became a chairman of the resulting corporation. The declining price of oil caused W to recalculate his business prospects. He sold the energy company for a bargain price but later cashed in on the stock shares he held.

In the mid 1980s the sometimes-wayward W reached a turning point in his personal and professional life. He decided to quit drinking altogether and turned toward the Christian faith. He became noticeably more serious and driven professionally. His father's decision to run for president in 1988 drew W to the challenge of national politics. W moved with his family to Washington, D.C., in the fall of 1987 to work on his father's successful campaign. Though W had no official campaign staff title, he was his father's most trusted confidant and a key point of contact for his colleagues. He also honed his speaking skills as the campaign's chief liaison to Christian conservatives.

On a roll after the 1988 election, W returned to Texas with a new dream. He solicited a group of wealthy investors to join him in purchasing the Texas Rangers professional baseball team. W served as the team's managing partner. He successfully leveraged the team's popularity to build his reputation among Texans and ultimately his own fortune when the team was sold in 1998.

With his father out of office, and the Texas Rangers doing well, W surprised his friends and family by running for governor of Texas in 1994. He defeated a popular Democrat incumbent to secure the office. Over the course of the next four years, his effective, easygoing nature made him one of the most popular big-state governors in the country. Even the state legislature, controlled by the opposing party, found him agreeable to work with. He was elected by a wide margin for a second term.

His impressive appeal in Texas and his national notoriety piqued the interest of the Republican Party's leadership. In June 1999, George W. Bush officially announced his intention to run for President of the United States. Billing himself as a "compassionate conservative," he was sworn in as the forty-third President of the United States in January 2001.[5]

Are great men born or is greatness thrust upon them? Similarly, are the wretched born into despair or are trying circumstances thrust upon them? We esteem grit and determination, celebrate fortune, deride an ugly twist of fate. Yet what determines the circumstances surrounding a life? The course and pace of the journey? The glory of the destination?

Choices.

The will to choose between the alternatives of life, the options one has before him, and persevere in those choices makes all the difference.

The road to the Presidency is paved with choices. Not all are born to wealth and privilege, as the brief histories of the last five U.S. presidents show. Carter was born into a farming family. Reagan came from working-class roots. The most prestigious candidate, of the five, George H. W. Bush faced the most daunting challenges as a pilot in World War II. All five suffered losses, all five tasted defeat.

Despite humble beginnings and recurring challenges, each of the very different men who eventually succeeded in becoming President of the United States were alike in some simple, yet profound, ways: they all had desire, they all had faith (in themselves and some higher plan), and they all had the will to choose, pursuing their dreams and persevering despite the obstacles.

The route to any worthwhile destination requires that you choose and persevere in your choice. Extraordinary journeys are guided by determined wills and determined choices.

Like the recounting of a man's (and possibly soon a woman's) rise to the Presidency, a fantastic journey is the power of an epic story fueled by the will of wise choices. Events are shaped by small decisions to act, to proceed. The events, taken together, form the grand mosaic that is a life well spent. Not a life of fear, but rather a life of trials and triumph.

Choose wisely, act and persevere; the reward of a life well lived is beyond measure.

Paradox of Purpose

Life has meaning. The meaning is beautiful in its simplicity, rich in its diversity, magnificent in its unity. Yet we often miss the beauty, the richness, the magnificence. The meaning of life is lost when sleep beckons and events sweep us up and consume our consciousness. It is then that the link between flesh and spirit is lost, and the observer becomes attached to, one with, the observed.

The purpose of life is to be — to journey, to observe, to experience. The journey is a dream, the separation from God an illusion. Each life gives the whole the opportunity to explore and experience part. We are in the Garden of Eden. We are in the ultimate playground, immersed in a landscape, part and

If I don't know where I'm going
Any road will do.

parcel of a grand collage. All that is has meaning in being — a grand purpose concealed in the apparent complexity of the environment. The culmination of the grand design is achieved, made possible, by small, obscure but nonetheless important contributions: "Every hair is counted." (Luke 12:7)

The world has a purpose and you have a place in the grand design, a place wholly reserved for you. You are a critical instrument in the symphony of life. Without you to play the note, make the instrument sing, the music is incomplete, less rich and textured, less fulfilled. Your reason for being — to play your note — conforms, fits into a greater purpose. The complex of seemingly disconnected and, what may appear to be conflicting or contradictory, purposes together weaves an extraordinary tapestry. Your life, individually, holds meaning that contributes to the whole. That contribution is being. Realizing you are not just the drama — awakening from the slumber to recognize a grand scheme — is the gift of grace in your life.

You Are Created and Creator

Blasphemy! Ah, but you have heard this before.

Somehow, deep within your being this claim rings true. You, we, all that is in this reality of forms, are creations. Creation originates from, is of, is — the source, the whole. We come from, are of, are, the whole. We have a connection to, are one with, the divine. Therefore though we accept the limitations of existence in this reality we are created from, but remain one with, the source. We are created in the flesh, yet we are simultaneously creator in spirit.

As created, we react to what we observe. We are immersed in the game. If you'll permit yet another analogy, we are on the field, pressed by an offense, attempting to turn the momentum and stem the tide. Through the ego we seek to take control of our destiny in the game, but the ego does not grasp the truth.

If you don't change course,
you'll get where you're headed.

Once we recognize and embrace our true nature we come to understand we are players on the field with the ability to manipulate the game, not through what we do on the field but through what we intend, desire, focus on (through spirit). We have the absolute ability to alter our perspective from the front line to the side line and influence the game, the field, the setting, the entire circumstance. The ego is content to struggle in the game, even while other options exist. We can, with surety, assume the role of the creator and create a new reality within bounds already set, limits agreed upon before we came into this reality, before we joined the game.

In the New Testament is found the notion of being "saved." Some interpret this as God bestowing favor on one who submits to the Provider's will. Others offer another perspective, a perspective of unity (creation and creator); being "saved" is awakening to the fact that you are one with creation and one with the source.

Being "saved" is recognizing life anew. If you accept the truth you are one with all that is, enduring and without need, you are "saved" then and there, here and now. You live from an unlimited, timeless perspective, safe and secure in the faith that no matter what happens in the world of form you exist beyond form — complete and whole — fulfilled and at peace. Wisdom has found its place. From this perspective you, an individual, on a journey through time and space, a journey replete with purpose, travel with surety that all that is, is good.

Exploring the New Testament further regarding being "saved," we find the early Christians struggled with how one is "saved" (the nature of ego is consistent through the ages in human experience). Some contend salvation is through works and is therefore under the individual's control.

Others contend that salvation is through grace, a gift from God outside the influence of the individual. The disparity in these views does not demand an "either or" as they are "both"

We can't see the end.
That is part of the fun,
The way it's meant to be.

possibilities from different perspectives, different levels of awareness. Both paths to salvation — by way of works or grace — are possible, are necessary, are real in this dream.

Through the centuries organized religions, dominated by the ego, have embraced the idea that life is form and that somehow we can and must buy our way out of form, pay a debt, redeem ourselves through penance. This perspective shackles the individual, lost in form, disconnected from the source, sinful and suffering, reliant on a universal benefactor, a power beyond form, to a god of power and might to save.

The gift of grace bestowed on an individual is the soul freeing realization that the world of form is not "it"; what we see is not all there is, and our physical senses do not give a complete picture. Grace is the gift of awakening to accept, believe, live knowing life is more than material surroundings and a series of events in time and space. Grace is the recognition that we are enduring, complete, and unified not in appearance but in purpose, in being, in spirit.

Someone can, within their nature, live a life connected to spirit, at peace with form, accepting of what is, and influencing by their focus on what becomes. These people are "saved" without an intellectual rationalization just an enduring, connected, vibrant faith. On the other side are the people who are seemingly disconnected from the source — the ones lost in everyday activities, seemingly alone and scared. To these people grace extends her hand, whispering, guiding, imploring at times, but never resting or sitting idly beside. Wisdom beckons, truth calls, grace whispers. The will to choose is our gift and our curse.

An essential point of the debate — "works versus grace" — is coming to grips with the notion that the intellect doesn't matter. Being saved through works can be understood from a perspective of recognizing the unity of the whole and choosing to experience fulfillment through works of sharing, of charity, of love. Similarly someone can just naturally, and in a state of

The one who endures to the end will be saved.

- MARK 13:13 -

sleep, conduct his life benevolently engaging in "good works" which, from an observer's perspective, are unifying, compassionate, and reinforcing, but the actor, the individual behaving generously, never recognizes his divinity in this existence. His slumber denies him the fulfillment and joy of recognizing that he is one with all that is — that he is on a journey of promise and potential. Yet, he is saved.

You Have a Choice

As both creation and creator we humans have unprecedented opportunity in this reality, in this playground — the promise and potential of life. We can choose what we will do, what we will be and, to a degree, what will be. And ultimately we choose when to go home.

The rules of the game are stacked in our favor (as crazy as that seems when we are lost in the illusion). Though we may see conflict and strife, disharmony and discord, those are the results of our perspective, the ego's need to judge, and the decision of the collective will on what to experience (the grand design). We can will another way.

You have a choice.

Contradiction seems rampant in this existence. We observe but often fail to see meaning, purpose, harmony, unity. The tides of change ebb and flow with a rhythmic persistence yet, somehow, we find ourselves adrift, lost at sea. We are imprisoned by our "human" nature, caught in the emotion of being; we succumb to the ego. The need to survive, the energy of emotion, and limitations of the intellect are overwhelmed by the complexity of the environment, the demands of the moment, the challenges of the flesh. Embracing the "world" view, we forget our "true" nature and come to accept and empower the belief that "It's me against the world."

Yet we have a choice.

God, give us grace to accept with serenity
the things that cannot be changed,
courage to change the things
which should be changed, and wisdom
to distinguish one from the other.

- THE SERENITY PRAYER -

Will is the capacity to choose rightly and persevere in our choosing until the smoke clears, the fog lifts, the clouds part — until the truth is revealed. You see, we are on a journey from the trifles of everyday existence to the exuberance of ultimate joy. Wisdom is the revelation, the realizing, the involuntary embracing of the truth that we are whole, complete, timeless and immortal; we are spirit on a human journey; we are observers of a vast illusion, at once rich in texture and diversity, alive and dynamic and yet simple in elegance and symmetry, graceful in bearing, profound in inspiration and grounded in direction.

Will

Fate or free will, choice or predestination; this debate that has raged since man has conceived himself separate from his surroundings and apparently confronted with options. Some say the script is written, that we are moving through the dream, experiencing the rush but not really choosing the course. Others contend that choices abound, options are infinite, that free will is the operative of this existence.

Scientists, exploring the nature of forces, have stumbled across the nearly infinite string of cause and effect — the consequence of every force is an incontrovertible result. Every "A" leads to a "B" leads to a "C" without deviation. The forces once set in motion are not to be deterred from their net effect. In this construct we have no room for choice. Cause and effect, and ultimately life, can be reduced to a mathematical equation (understandably with nearly infinite variables nonetheless) — forces moving to a predetermined quotient.

Without much consideration, in the day-to-day reality of life we believe we have choices. For heaven's sake we can choose coffee, tea, milk or juice for breakfast; beer, wine, or schnapps, for that matter; or nothing at all. We can choose to wear blue,

Do not despair
Nor forsake this life
Though it be temporary
And the beat be fleeting
It is not for naught
Nor is death an end
Your life is a gift
A chance to laugh and cry
Dance and sing
Struggle and fall
Dream and try
Do not let the opportunity pass you by.
Join the dance
Lead the song
Dare great deeds
Pass life and love along
The opportunity before
Like a springtime bud
Will bloom and flower
Fade and die
This truth fuels passion
Inspires action
Idle not on the sideline of life
Loose your spirit and fly.

red, yellow, green, a turtleneck or cutoffs, a beret or bonnet. We can work in industry, government, services, manufacturing. We can live here, live there, or live nowhere at all. The choices seem never-ending.

Those choices, however, are not so much endless as they are meaningless. Like a tree that falls in the forest, without someone to bestow meaning, no meaning exists.

Some conceive of no beauty, no truth, without conscious choice. For without choice, without free will, all is for naught. Without choice, life would be a horrible hoax perpetrated on defenseless, ignorant automatons existing under the illusion, the colorful construct, of purpose. Without free will, life truly is the divine comedy. Yet, as we've said so many times, we know there exists something more than the intellect can corral, some things beyond our understanding; free will fits in this category.

The scientific recognition of the immutability of a force set in motion, however disputed, may be true. True or not, it is not relevant for the lives we lead and the reality we experience. The argument for fate, as rational as it may be, discounts the complex motif and the awe and wonder and richness of the infinitely interacting forces and the influence of powers outside the dimension of this known reality.

What we seek is not an intellectual understanding of the means of this illusion but rather the truth of who and what we are. We seek to know the truth to embrace our true nature and thereby arrive at the pure joy of being.

If this reality is not the ultimate reality, if we are in this world in experience only, immersed in the illusion, it stands to reason that the powers in another dimension can influence what happens, what appears here. If we further subscribe to the belief that though we seem to live here, ultimately we are not of here, we can begin to grasp we have a means to influence this reality. We have will.

Seek help through patience and prayer; God stands alongside the patient! . . . Patient people who say, whenever disaster strikes them, "We are God's, and are returning to Him!" Such will be granted their prayers by their Lord as well as mercy. Those are guided!

- QUR'AN 2:153-157 -

Will is determination, desire, resolve, want, wish and longing all rolled up into the person we recognize as "me." Will is the power of focus, the force of intent, the motive of prayer. Will is the impulse to change, whether that impulse is to fulfill a physical need, scratch an itch, or realize a life goal. Will is the decision point — the capacity to recognize want, determine options, and make choices.

Often we seem to go through life without stumbling across or pausing at the decision point. Sometimes life seems to happen so fast we act without hesitating to consider that we even have options. In fact, most often we act, and only afterward rationalize a reason for the choice we appear to have made. A life without choosing is a life on autopilot. It is a life either completely dominated by ego, a life lost in the illusion, unconscious of options, or a life so accepting and in harmony with spirit that each new day is a joy to behold.

While I strive for and hope for a life in harmony with spirit, unencumbered by the joust with the intellect or the intimidation of the ego, I find myself often lost in the maze. I struggle with the ego and get swept up by emotion and feeling, sometimes with ill results. To put it in a dualistic way, every day is either a day of revelation (a day of discovery and progress) or, as in the Bill Murray movie, it's groundhog day, repeating itself over and over again.

Will is the aspect of each of our beings that recognizes, sometimes in the most subtle and obscure ways, that we have options for suffering or profit.

Will also is the battleground, the point of coming together of spirit and ego to wrestle over and determine a choice, to set a course, to change a mood, to plot an outcome. Will is the decision point, the place to claim or abdicate responsibility. Will determines ultimately the experience of joy or despair, acceptance or rejection of every event, every action, every moment. Will is the power to choose.

We want to die.
Let the story of me, the contents of your mind (ego) die.
Sense of self is tied up in the story of me.
I am incomplete;
I never have enough in the story of me.

- Eckhart Tolle -

If will is the capacity to choose — the notion you have some degree of control over your journey — my prayer for you asks that your being be infused with the will, the desire, to choose rightly and for every seemingly unsatisfying outcome persevere in choosing again. For ultimately you and I are one as are you one with all things. When the veil of misunderstanding is finally torn, you will recognize and appreciate that the pain, the suffering, the insecurity were all for naught. You are safe, secure, whole and beyond harm, secure in the warm embrace of a loving peace.

The key to will is orientation. Are we disposed to choose rightly, choose wisely? Are we headed in the right direction? Are we listening to the right guides? Or are we undermining our own progress by submitting to the ego? Denying responsibility for our lives? And disregarding the road signs and messengers of truth?

The cost of heading the wrong way, of denying responsibility, or disregarding the road signs and messengers of truth is only time — time spent suffering. The choices we make, the energy we invoke, the game we play is not without consequence. We are created, and as such fill our roles in a story much grander than the plot of our individual lives. At the same time we are creator. As such we can choose to accelerate the plot line, manipulate the story, for good or ill. No matter what we rationalize in our intellect there is no escaping; in life, choices matter. Will wisely.

I have but one choice,
In the unfolding symphony of creation;
Play my note;
If in harmony, play strong,
If in discord,
The beauty of the symphony
Will engulf my note,
Gently reshape its tone,
And in God's time,
Conjoin it with the beautiful, enduring,
Symphony of love;
Either live by faith,
In peace and joy;
Or resist love,
And struggle seemingly alone;
I have but one choice.

Will to choose; to persevere

✦ Life has purpose. ✦

✦ We are created and creator. ✦

✦ You have a choice. ✦

✦ Will to choose rightly and persevere. ✦

In the end — in both the grand design and the sometimes monotonous details of everyday existence — purpose unfolds. The distance from fragile form, inept intellect, and pliable will to pure joy, divine love, and ultimate fulfillment is the width and breadth of the ego. Life has meaning. You have a purpose to fulfill. Accept your purpose. Meet your destiny joyfully.

Puppets on a string, we live in shadows vainly interpreting reflections on a wall. When we yield to fear we hide from the light of revelation, from realizing that we are more than we seem. In the world of form, as creation, we lack understanding. We grovel over the indulgences of ego — competing to succeed, competing to survive. The truth is, we need not live this way.

While experiencing this reality of polar opposites we can seize upon the truth. While we are in this world, we are not of this world, and therefore do not have to succumb to the will and fear of the ego. Your nature is divine. While in this creation you have the capacity to create. You are creator. And as creator you can choose how you navigate this illusion. You have a choice.

Will is the element of character that merges feelings of yearning (wants, needs, desires) with recognizable options and chooses. Each choice is either guided in harmony with life's purpose (right choice) or influenced by a scheming, power-hungry ego. Every choice is an opportunity to choose wisely in harmony with the grand design or an ego-grounded choice doomed to lead through suffering to the same point of decision again. Will to choose rightly and persevere. Joy awaits.

Yet not my will, but yours be done.

Pray for wisdom.
If you are wise, your life will be full.

If you cannot grasp wisdom,
Pray for courage.
Courage to let go leads to wisdom.

If you cannot claim courage,
Pray for strength.
Strength to overcome leads to courage.

If you cannot summon strength,
Pray for will.
Will rightly employed leads to strength.

Be and Become

The way is easy, the burden light.
- MATTHEW 11:30 -

Acres of Diamonds[6]

In an ancient land with a rich culture, not far from the Indus River, once lived an old and noble Persian by the name of Al Hafed. The magnificent land was marked by million-year-old caves in hardened rocks, towering forests, lofty hills, green fertile fields, deep blue lakes, winding rivers and a seascape of golden beaches. Here Al Hafed owned a very large farm with orchards, grain fields and gardens. He was a contented and wealthy man — contented because he was wealthy, and wealthy because he was contented.

One day there visited this old farmer an ancient Buddhist priest, Inzan. Inzan sat down by Al Hafed's fire to warm himself. As the night grew dark and deep, he told that old farmer how this world of ours was made.

The priest said that this world was once a mere bank of fog. The Almighty thrust his finger into the bank of fog and then began slowly to swirl his finger around and gradually to increase the speed of his finger until at last he whirled that bank of fog into a solid ball of fire. The ball of fire went rolling through the universe, burning its way through other cosmic banks of fog, until it condensed the moisture without. The moisture fell in floods of rain upon the heated surface and cooled the outward crust. Then the internal flames burst through the cooling crust and threw up the mountains and made the hills and the valleys of this wonderful world of ours.

The priest went on to explain how rocks, metals and precious gems were formed. If the internal melted mass burst out and cooled very quickly it became granite; that which cooled less quickly became silver; and less quickly, gold; and after gold, diamonds were made.

Said Inzan, "A diamond is a congealed drop of sunlight."

This is a scientific truth. Diamond is pure carbon — actually deposited sunlight.

Inzan declared that a diamond is the last and highest of God's mineral creations, as a woman is the last and highest of God's animal creations. Maybe that is the reason why the two have such an affinity for each other.

Inzan told Al Hafed that if he had a handful of diamonds he could purchase a whole country, and with a mine of diamonds he could place his children upon thrones through the influence of their great wealth.

Al Hafed heard all about diamonds and how much they were worth. He went to his bed that night a poor man — not that he had lost anything, but poor because he was discontented and discontented because he thought he was poor.

Al Hafed thought: "I want a mine of diamonds!" So he lay awake all night.

Eager to acquire diamonds Al Hafed awakened the priest out of his dreams early in the morning.

Al Hafed said to the priest, "Will you tell me where I can find diamonds?"

Inzan, shaking the slumber from his head replied, "Diamonds? What do you want with diamonds?"

"I want to be immensely rich," implored Al Hafed, "but I don't know where to go."

"Well," said Inzan "if you will find a river that runs over white sand between high mountains, in those sands you will always see diamonds."

"Do you really believe that there are such rivers?" asked Al Hafed.

"Plenty of them, plenty of them; all you have to do is just go and find them. Then you will have your diamonds."

Al Hafed's desire had burned through the night and now consumed him, he hastened to conclude, "I will go."

Al Hafed sold his farm, collected his money at interest, left his family in the charge of a neighbor, and went away in search of diamonds. He was a man of action, fueled by desire. He had the will of purpose, the strength of means, and the courage of conviction. Al Hafed was sure of his knowledge and confident in his ability.

Al Hafed began very properly — at mythical mountains in Africa.

The existence of snow-capped mountains near the equator in Africa seemed preposterous. Yet Al Hafed put faith in the rumor of these mountains (which a Greek geographer, Ptolemy, later named Lunae Montes or Mountains of the Moon) and persisted. However the search for the Mountains of the Moon proved nearly futile. That was until one day when Al Hafed happened to be in the right place at the right time. Normally cloud cover obscured the mountains from onlookers, but on this day the clouds began to dissipate and Al Hafed caught a glimpse of a group of snow-capped mountains. Al Hafed found the Mountains of the Moon, known to the native Africans as "Ruwenzori" or "Rainmaker."

To this day, the Mountains of the Moon still maintain an aura of mystery. Lying just north of the equator, the Ruwenzori Mountains provide a natural barrier between Uganda and the Democratic Republic of Congo. The mountains stretch some eighty miles and are about thirty miles wide. They are different from most mountain ranges in East Africa in that they are not of volcanic origin. Rather they are a huge block of the earth's crust that was thrust upward millennia ago by enormous geologic pressures. The mountains reach a peak of 16,763 feet. They are, however, rarely visible to onlookers as a result of the mists and clouds that enshroud them.

The Ruwenzori Mountains were so named because of the abundance of snow and rain that occur in their vicinity. The dry season is, in fact, only slightly drier than the wet season. The landscape is covered by thick vegetation. Into this dangerous, forbidding terrain Al Hafed ventured. For years, he traversed the slopes, ascended the heights, and probed the depths for his elusive prize — tears of God.

Scouting the mountains, Al Hafed passed through tropical rain forests and crossed countless rivers. At altitude he was rewarded with stunning views down into the valleys below. He trudged up and down through tussock grass and heath trees. He encountered waist-deep mud and negotiated perilous glaciers. Try as he might, the mountains never revealed the trophy for which he toiled. The only tears he found were the tears he shed from the pain of his struggle. Undaunted, however, Al Hafed headed north.

Al Hafed skirted the Mediterranean searching the coastal and inner plains of Palestine. He explored the fertile deltas and rummaged the river basins into the rugged hills and mountains. Al Hafed's quest brought him across large rocky terraces populated by olive, almond, and apple trees. He traversed fields of wheat, barley, and lentils that reminded him of the farm he had abandoned and the family he had left behind. He ventured on, the years wearing on his body, the disappointment wearing on his spirit.

Al Hafed pushed north, wandering on into Europe. He probed every river, he encountered, looking hopefully for white sands. He roamed every mountain range he caught sight of. From every disheartening crest he spied further features to explore. With each passing season he grew more disillusioned. His dream failed.

At last, when his money was all spent, and he was in rags, wretchedness, and poverty, Al Hafed stood on the shore of a bay in Spain. A tidal wave came rolling in through the Pillars of Hercules (the fabled promontories at the eastern end of the Mediterranean set by Hercules as a memorial of his labor of seizing the cattle of the three-bodied giant Geryon). The poor, afflicted, suffering man could not resist the awful temptation to cast himself into that incoming tide. Al Hafed, once a prominent, wealthy, noble landowner, sank beneath a wave's foaming crest, never to rise in this life again.

But what of Al Hafed's treasure? Soon after Al Hafed had begun his quest his successor, the new owner of Al Hafed's farm, Behrouz, led his camel out into the garden to drink. As that camel put its nose down into the clear water of the garden brook Behrouz noticed a curious flash of light from the sands of the shallow stream. Reaching in he pulled out a black stone having an eye of light that reflected all the colors of the rainbow. He took that curious pebble into the house and left it on the mantel, then went on his way, forgetting all about it.

A few days after that, this same old priest, Inzan, who told Al Hafed how diamonds were made, came in to visit Al Hafed's successor Behrouz. When Inzan saw that flash of light from the mantel he rushed up proclaiming, "Here is a diamond — here is a diamond! Has Al Hafed returned?"

Behrouz looked on calmly, "No, no; Al Hafed has not returned and that is not a diamond; that is nothing but a stone. I found it right out here in the garden."

"But I know a diamond when I see one," Inzan replied. "That is a diamond!"

Then together they rushed to the garden and stirred up the white sands with their fingers. They found diamonds more beautiful, more valuable, than the first. Together they discovered the diamond mines of Golconda, the most magnificent diamond mines in all the history of mankind.

The mines of Golconda, found in the garden of a once contented man who died despairing, produced the great Kohinoor diamond in England's crown jewels and the largest crown diamond on earth in Russia's crown jewels, and the Hope diamond among countless other gems.

Had Al Hafed remained at home and dug in his own cellar or in his own garden, instead of wretchedness, starvation, poverty and death in a strange land, he would have had "acres of diamonds."

For every acre, yes, every shovelful of Al Hafed's old farm afterward revealed the gems which since have decorated the crowns of royalty. Al Hafed possessed untold wealth if only he had searched in his own backyard.

"Acres of Diamonds" is a great story illustrating just how often our focus is misplaced. Al Hafed, a landowner, was wealthy and contented. He had it all until, learning of the magnificence and power of diamonds, he decided he did not have enough. He risked everything searching vainly for a treasure that had been his all along. Al Hafed literally walked away from acres of diamonds and ended his life in despair.

Is this a true story? You bet. It's a story that has been lived millions of times by millions of people, who abandon their greatest assets to search for something they mistakenly believe they lack.

We search frantically — in some cases for what, we do not know — a place for "me" in this world, a place yet to find. Some people wallow in the despair of longing. Others ache with a sense of emptiness, craving something more. In response to the ache, many shackle themselves to the will of the ego. In this game, success, fulfillment, happiness, are in distant lands, beyond the next river, over the next hill, always around the next elusive corner. The draw, the elixir of our search is: fortune, fame, love, security, power — attributes we believe we do not possess.

The moral of "Acres of Diamonds" is a message that rings true to each of us. We travelers — adventurers, ordinary people living ordinary lives — have what we need to succeed in this life. We need not covet something elusive, we need only recognize and appreciate the treasure we possess — our acres of diamonds.

The distance from despair to fulfillment, from longing to abundance, from sorrow to celebration, is a realization in our mind. *Promise and Potential* is an intellectualized account of an experiential journey from wherever you are today to pure happiness and pure joy.

Wisdom recognizes our acres of diamonds. Yet if our vision is clouded, we can call on courage and strength and will to help us find our way. The story of every life, though perceived as a disparate trek, is actually an element of an intricately woven tapestry. We are not poor, we are not separate, we are not alone. Deciding to join the chorus and being content with our role makes all the difference.

Now let's turn to practical means to reorient our focus, and exert and invoke the power of wisdom through the habits of choice.

We despair in the game of hide and seek;
We search unceasingly,
To find God hidden in plain sight,
Surrounding us,
Protecting us,
Loving us,
In spite of our foolishness.

Where along the Path?

We've been talking about an experience we call life. We perceive life as a journey, a passage through time, a voyage from one place and time to another. Yet every journey begins from the same place, and every journey has as its purpose to achieve the same end. The place to begin is where you are now; the purpose is to achieve salvation.

Presumably, if you've stayed with me this far, you have a sense your experience of life could be much more than it has been. It can be! What you think you lack you can, in fact, find. The place to start is where you are. The place to look for the answers is where the answers are found — within. There is no other door, no other route home.

Our lives we fill with questions. The questions substitute for getting on with the real task of going home, of embracing God. By posing questions and pursuing "new" answers we think we will find a reasoned way home, a way and a means that conforms to this life. We search and search because the answer that is before us does not satisfy the ego, does not conform to the rules of the reality we perceive ourselves caught in.

Well here are the questions that matter, and the answers that matter.

Who?	You
What?	Attain Salvation
When?	Now
Where?	Within
How?	By Forgiving — Letting Go
Why?	Because unimaginable joy is your destiny

Now the task is not to answer questions but is rather to get on with the work of journeying home. The challenge is to do

Cry if you might,
Wail if you must,
But stand not in the path of brave pioneers.
Comfort is not their calling,
Appeasement not their way.
Complaints and derision,
Never justification.

Freedom and fulfillment come,
Not on the easy road,
But by overcoming fear, hatred, anger.

The challenge:
To contribute something positive,
With the gift of life.
Recourse:
To retreat to a hovel of comfort,
A vane and shallow harbor,
Worshiping idols of wealth and status,
Where bondage and death await.

the simple, but paradoxically difficult, single task of life — letting go the ego, dissolving the illusion.

You have a will for this purpose — it's your desire to change. You have a wellspring of strength, from a source you cannot see but know is real. You have the courage to proceed one step at a time. With surety you will arrive with the wise — recognizing your true self — one with God.

This reality is dynamic, constantly changing. We are immersed in creation, immersed in the journey of life. Ultimately, all is illusion. The gift of free will, though not as broad as we like to think, is the key to the choice we must make, the option we must ultimately pursue. We can exercise our free will to live and suffer in the illusion or to journey to our true home. We have two well defined choices: 1. Embrace truth, go with the flow, accept, create, and rejoice; or 2. Embrace ego, resist, compete, and survive in the illusion. If we choose wisely, we ally with truth and forego a separate will, a separate "I." If we choose poorly we must harden ourselves for a lonely journey dominated by ego, flush with fear.

What we believe matters. For the origin of the word "belief" offers a telling verse. Belief is a compound word with parts synonymous to: "Be" is "By" and "Lief" is "Live." Taken together, the meaning of something we "Believe" in is something we "Live By." Further examination leads us to: "Be" is "Exist" and "Lief" is "Full of Life." Hence someone who "Believes" "Exists Full of Life." Finally, "Be" may mean "By or In the Presence of" and "Lief" may mean "Love." In this definition we can say "Belief" means "In the Presence of Love." Accepting the meaning of the word, then, beliefs determine a worldview inextricably linked to how one lives. Rational explanations (or intellectual fabrications) notwithstanding, beliefs organize our lives; we do what we believe.

What do you really believe? You can determine this only by observing how you live, how you respond to others, how

Judge not, lest ye be judged

- LUKE 6:37 -

you respond to the world around you, and what you do. Is it time to change?

The only thing people prefer to the way things are is the way they were. We seek security in the past and attempt to prolong the glory of past triumphs. Instead, remember, begin where you are now. Though you may temporarily succumb to doubt, recognize that progress in this reality always involves resistance and always involves risk. It is time to act; it is time to change beliefs, to be what you really are, to become whole.

The tools for this process of change are first, humility (judge not, accept) and finally, focus (in silence identify truth, then let go/forgive). In the end, you will live a full life unencumbered by fear, guilt, anger or remorse. In silence the Holy Spirit is revealed. Through kindness you discipline yourself to dissolve the illusion and journey home. It is time to be and become.

Judge Not

"A man of supreme faith in God waited and watched as torrents of rain fell raising the nearby river. In a few days the river overflowed its banks. The water began to flood the man's house. After three days of fighting off flood waters a neighbor in a canoe came by to ask our hero if he needed help getting to dry land. No, the man insisted, God would care for him. He sent the Good Samaritan on his way. The water continued to rise, until the man was trapped on the second story of his house. Within hours a speedboat came by, its driver offered the man a lift to drier, safer ground. Again the man rejected the offer; God would save him. The waters continued to rise, forcing the man to scramble to his roof. As daylight broke after a miserable night a helicopter flew in, dropping a line to pull the man to safety. Again the man refused, claiming God would rescue him. Finally the water collapsed the house, drowning our would-be hero in the torrent. Our hero, upon seeing God in

The moment is as near as now,
The goal as close as here,
Thy will be done.

Heaven, lamented, "Lord I put my faith in you to rescue me." God looked at the man with pity and replied, "Well, heck, I sent a canoe, a speedboat, and a helicopter — what more did you expect?'"

The first sin of ego is hubris, arrogance. The arrogance of ego is to insist, "I know best." "I know what is right." "I know the answers." "I know the way." "And the world will conform to my will."

We punish ourselves through our pride and hubris as we seek rather to be "right" than to be "happy"; to get "our way" rather than to "have peace"; to be "vindicated" rather than exist in "harmony."

We judge by appearance, by demeanor, by expression, by every sense and faculty. Every judgment is an exultation of "I" the "ego" over the "other." We seek power, we yearn for control. We feel powerful in our self-righteousness. But we remain lost and alone in a divided, dangerous reality, a reality of our own making.

To be and become what we truly are — children of God — embraced by the Creator's immeasurable love, we **MUST** release the comfort of judging. As we journey through the illusion of life, we must forego the ego's attempt to seize power and bestow position by condemning individuals or circumstances. This is no easy task — the ego is a crafty force. But through personal vigilance, you can master the ego. Discipline your need to judge.

Accept

To succeed in mastering the ego — triumphing over the illusion — we must accept two seemingly paradoxical conditions: 1. The master plan is beyond our understanding, is greater than our intellect; and 2. We are totally responsible for our lives, all that happens, all that is.

Do not lay up an earthly treasure...
Do not worry about the cares of this life...
Seek first his kingship, his way of holiness,
Then all things will be given you besides.

- MATTHEW 6 -

This leaves us quite a quandary. We can't understand the plan — the workings, purpose and destiny of this reality— yet we are totally and completely responsible for our experience of it. This is a difficult proposition at best for our limited minds. We are tossed and buffeted by the waves, the winds, and the passions of this existence. Our bodies have limited control over the circumstances of this physical reality. Yet, in truth, this "reality" — the waves, winds, and emotions — is only a dream.

Accept total responsibility for all that is and all that happens and realize the truth; none of it is real, none of it matters. Saying this (or reading this, or writing this, for that matter) is one thing; believing, and therefore living it, is another. To go from the skepticism, fear, and self-righteousness of the ego to the truth requires conditioning the self to step back from the emotion of the moment and recognize and realize circumstances are what they are and that is all. Every moment, every action, every interaction is an opportunity to disempower the ego and empower spirit, to learn, to move closer to ultimate reality — to move closer to God.

What to do is accept that all is right with the world — it's okay. Rain, wind, snow; rich, poor; educated, uneducated, it's okay. The circumstances of life are neither "someone's" nor "the system's" fault. There is no victim. There is no one to blame. This lesson is offered until the wisdom of this truth is accepted. We are not separate; we are masters of our fate.

Our choice is to accept or resist — to be in harmony (at peace) or conflict (the ego's temporary illusion of power). Ultimately, the end is not in doubt; we choose the amount of pain suffered in the illusion as we journey to wholeness. The struggle is only and forever in the mind.

What is, is. For what will be you have two choices: go with the ego or go with God. Accept the master plan; humbly rejoice in every circumstance as awakening your responsibility to choose.

Salvation is:
To see your face in that of your brother.

Then will you realize you are one.

Let Go

Jesus said, "Oh weak in faith, stop worrying. Your heavenly Father knows what you need." God's plan works; yours does not. Align yourself with God's plan. The challenge is to not automatically fall victim to the ego. You must listen for the still small voice within. By rejecting the ego you open yourself to the Holy Spirit, to the divine plan.

Listen, plan, act, but do not attach yourself to outcomes. Let go of the outcome. Detach yourself from the details. Anxiety over outcomes is the realm of the ego. If the circumstance involves power and control, it's of the ego. The ego's main tool is fear. Let go — don't involve yourself in fear.

In this modern world of six and a half billion people there is only you. The masses are here to help **you** achieve salvation. Everyone else is here for **you**. Now, society should be running smoothly like water blending together in a stream. Instead, society often is more like rocks banging and grinding and scraping along. Your vision is not yet clear, your way not yet pure. You are resisting. You must learn to act like water, be the water, and accept the rocks — not for obstacles to confront but for rough edges to polish.

Let go of the anchor; it only draws you to new depths. Let go of the illusion; it only leads to regret. Like the monkey with its paw trapped in the jar, only by releasing its grip will it gain freedom. Choose freedom over bondage — release your grip. Let go; give it over to spirit.

You must let go of the blame, the fear, and the guilt. What you cling to holds you back. In truth, you are immersed in light. The truth surrounds you. You are immersed in God as if you were submerged in water; you breathe God, feel God, experience God, yet still your ego denies that God exists. Your ego asks you to choose the lonely way. Lift the veil of the illusion

Forgiving leads to unity,
Leads to joy.

and in so doing reveal that you are home, now, in the arms of God, enfolded in love. Accept this truth.

Let go of the fabricated faults, the perceived injustice, the self-imposed obstacles. It has been said that the greatest calamity of man is that he is ruled by the mind. It is time for you to give up the rule of the mind and instead let the spirit rule. The ego seeks to hold you back. Let go.

Forgive

Wherever the ego looks, it sees conflict and division, pain and oppression. The ego's tools are blame and fear. To move from the tempest to the calm, from trial to peace, from guilt to innocence, we must invest the talent and energy at our disposal to recognize the world for what it is — illusion. To embrace the true, enduring reality we must forgive those we perceive who trespass against us and we must forgive the circumstances and events we perceive to conspire against us. By letting go of the conflict of the illusion we ultimately forgive ourselves.

Remember, "I am responsible." And "Forgiveness comes from forgiving."

Life is to be lived. Whether we tend to believe we are journeying through the valley of death, our final destination is the safety of a warm embrace and loving home. To get to that destination do not squander your life, nor spend it frivolously; invest what you have in the lives of others. To invest life, you must be able to share unencumbered by guilt. For peace to reign, you must forgive — all and always.

Today is not life in the fast lane; it is life in the oncoming lane. The ego puts us in the oncoming lane and accelerates life so that we find it difficult to hear the still small voice calling out to guide the way, the voice calling us home. We must undo the ego's obstacles to recognize God. And the biggest obstacles to truth are the perceptions in our mind we have been wronged

Love is patient; love is kind.
Love is not jealous, it does not put on airs,
it is not snobbish.
Love is never rude, it is not self-seeking,
it is not prone to anger; neither does it
brood over injuries.
Love does not rejoice in what is wrong but
rejoices in the truth.
There is no limit to love's forbearance, to its trust,
its hope, its power to endure.
Love never fails...
Faith, hope, love abide these three but the
greatest of these is love.

- 1 CORINTHIANS -

or we are unworthy of going home. Both these misperceptions (blame and fear) require true forgiveness.

Ultimately, we have to unleash ourselves from the bondage of this world. The journey from sleep to awakening is made in small steps. We learn to forgive by not judging, by accepting responsibility for all we experience, and by letting go of perceived hurts and perceived injustices. You see, if this life is an illusion, then so are our perceptions of injustice. There is no one to blame and nothing to fear.

Forgiving is giving peace, allowing a smile, inviting laughter despite the circumstances. You are not separate from your creator. You are not alone. You are one — whole, complete, powerful, and loving. You forgive yourself in the same measure as how you forgive others.

Love

Paul's epistle to the Corinthians (facing page) is one of the most beautiful descriptions of what love is. Yet love is still an elusive concept in our dualistic reality. When we say "God is love," we merge together two equally mystifying concepts. The concepts are too grand, all-encompassing, universally unifying and unidimensionally perfect. The point is, both "God" and "love" defy definition. The best we can hope for, and in fact enjoy in our unenlightened state, is to experience but a slight taste, gather an incomplete glimpse, and inhale a partial breath of a truly transcendent, awe-inspiring, reality beyond description.

So, how then do we make love real in this constrained experience? By enlarging ourselves to grow into the majesty that is love and by learning and living the universal traits of a unified whole in simple yet substantive ways.

We open to spirit and open to truth by listening to the still small voice; by assuming responsibility for all aspects of our

Even at the level of the most casual encounter,
it is possible for two people
to lose sight of separate interests,
if only for a moment.
That moment will be enough,
salvation has come.

- A Course In Miracles -

lives; by humbly acting in this world, open to the intentions of spirit, accepting of the circumstances we confront; and moving ever forward toward the goal that spirit intends us to seek: peace, joy, fulfillment, unity.

As we are in a dualistic state, we in effect act to oppose those forces that push, pull, or cajole us from our divine inheritance. We must resist the ego, not by force, but by releasing any desire to affix blame and in so doing forgive what we, from our limited perspectives, believe are sins against us or our self-righteous truth.

Love is gentle, love is kind, but love is not weak. Love is unwavering in its pursuit of truth. Submitting to ego (whether one's own or the ego of another) is not love. As the experience of God is beyond this reality, the way to love is through the guide of spirit. The truth of which, the authenticity of which, one can only measure within.

Faith is the acceptance of truth unseen. Hope is a sense that what is to come is beneficial. Love is the conviction of faith and hope in action. You are in a dynamic world of change. Love is the small obligation of your spirit to manifest positive outcomes. In so doing, you find your way home.

Live

Who am I, and why am I here?

These are basic, yet profound, questions, ones that we rarely address as we struggle to earn a living, complete an education, raise a family, succeed, survive. We work to provide lifestyle. We devote time and energy to economic pursuits; athletic endeavors; social engagements; entertainment. When do we have time to address these questions? Are there answers?

I offer for your consideration this idea: we are beings in a dynamic, compelling world. Though this is but an illusion, we

One life, well lived, changes the world!

are lost in the illusion and to find our way out we must act. We must live.

Every obstacle, every challenge, every experience, is an opportunity to find the right path, to journey one step closer to home. Life is for the living. Though you are not of this world you are in it. Your quest is not to succumb to the lure of the ego but rather to use your energy, your opportunity, your circumstance, to realize wisdom. You are to grow, to learn, and to teach, for the torch we hold for others shows us the way ahead.

The ultimate objective, for all of God's children, is to return home. Our destiny is salvation. To return to God, to achieve this goal, we have energy and will, strength and courage, and the wisdom of spirit as a guide. The lessons of life are expressed in the dynamic motion and energy of change. In this world we cannot stay still; we either surge forward or fall back. We must choose, we must act, we must live.

The relevance, beauty, and inspiration of the Bible story is not in telling a tale of an ancient people, their journey to a new land, and the promise of new life. Rather, the beauty and truth of the Bible story is that those accounts are the narrative of your life and mine. We are the souls leaving the garden, facing danger, losing our way, being bound in slavery and through faith and perseverance finding the way out and journeying to the Promised Land. We have to see beyond the dirt and rocks; the laws and the labels; the hunger and the strife; and recognize the truth. Don't fear this life nor look for truth in the material world. The Holy Spirit guides us to find truth within. Live life with zest and gusto. Live life for the adventure it is meant to be.

When you rule your mind,
you rule your world.

- Bill Provost -

Be and Become: Recognizing Promise, Fulfilling Potential

✦ Start from where you are; find the answers within. ✦

✦ Judge not, nor affix blame. ✦

✦ Accept responsibility to change what you can — yourself. ✦

✦ Let go of the ego and the fear it employs. ✦

✦ Forgive all perceived transgressions to release yourself. ✦

✦ Love unconditionally to grow toward God. ✦

Live with abandon. Life is intended to be a journey of joy.

Master the Half Dozen for success.

1. Live each moment.
2. Listen — pay attention to the still small voice within.
3. Control self (accept, let go, forgive) — master the ego; free yourself by going with the flow of the divine plan.
4. Eliminate fear.
5. Act on faith.
6. Stay the course.

This is but a restatement and summary of *Promise & Potential:* Live wisely, courageously, strongly, and by your will persevere.

Implement Simple Measures to Convert the Half Dozen

Focus on now (accept, reserve judgment).

Reflect before acting (pray; meditate; center; listen) — don't let emotions sweep you into bondage.

Observe fear.

Orient in the right direction.

Take the next step on faith.

Will consistently and persevere (discipline).

Your life becomes what you think.

- Marcus Aurelius -

If the inertia of change seems overwhelming and hardly possible for you to overcome, remember that you have been given other people, all circumstances, and the entire universe so as not to become distracted with self, self-absorbed, trapped by ego. Make it your mission to help yourself by assisting those around you to see the truth, grasp the truth, and in so doing head home. By mastering thought, by focusing your mind, all things are possible.

A Course In Miracles states, "It takes great learning to understand that all things, events, encounters and circumstances are helpful." Correcting others is of the ego. The Holy Spirit does not recognize fault or error, because the Holy Spirit understands the ego is folly. Humility, not arrogance, is the only way.

We often are left to wonder, "If it is true we are here to help others, what exactly are the others here for?" Wisdom realizes by forgiving we free ourselves. Forgive, let perceived transgressions go. Live in harmony with spirit. As the population grows, think of it as increasing opportunities for forgiveness — for giving, sharing, loving. We need each other. Each has special gifts. If we cooperate with each other in creation, together we lift the veil of illusion and come to realize oneness.

The essence of our being is awareness. We create, observe, and experience this reality. To change it requires our contribution. We contribute through intention. We change the world of effects in the realm of cause. And we are guided to the realm of cause by spirit. To journey in spirit requires faith. We exercise faith in quiet contemplation. The essence of prayer is faith. The essence of meditation is faith. The essence of intuition is faith. Believe! Energize your faith. Listen to spirit and act.

Bondage and salvation are both from within. Accept total responsibility for your life, both successes and failures.

Ultimately, your task is to return to God, to let go of the illusion and be whole. Life is simple: what we give, we get. We create our own experience, our own reality. We are responsible

Life is to experience;
Distinct and apart from the whole;
You have a mission,
To be a light in the darkness,
To be a cheerleader,
To engage in the fray,
To offer a hand,
To offer a smile,
To always point the way.

for changing it. You are responsible both for what is and how you react to what is. The world will change only if and when you do! We are children of God — one, whole, and complete, now and eternal. We lack nothing, we fear nothing, we accept and know what is. We live, we love, we are.

"I am the way, the truth and the life…" Do we get it or did we miss it? The truth and wisdom of Jesus' words are as valid and timeless now as when spoken 2,000 years ago. The way, truth, and life are a realization that we are connected to all people, to all creatures, to all things, timeless, immortal and complete. We are not lost and alone. We need only recognize and embrace the spirit of truth to awaken to a new life, to rise anew.

Jesus understood, as do all enlightened teachers, we are of one, in all, of all. We are not entombed in time or space but can transcend the boundaries we cling to so adamantly in this life. Through the still small voice we are called home.

God has endless love and compassion for those who believe they are not with him, but rather are lost in the illusion of their choice. He calls out, he lights a flame, he waits patiently, joyfully, and without fail.

The way and the reality of bliss are with and in us, of us, here and now today, in this instant, regardless of the circumstances of the physical manifestations of experience. Our lives can change in an instant — this instant, if we awaken to the spirit that is love, that is God, that is all, that is us, now. Jesus came so that we might have life and have it abundantly. The choice, by the grace of God, is ours to make. God grant you the wisdom to see, hear, and understand. If you embrace the truth, the truth will set you free. You will experience life to its fullest.

Using our theme — wisdom, courage, strength, will— I offer versions of our *Promise & Potential* prayer. Choose one that speaks to your heart. We truly are blessed – recognize this promise and fulfill your potential.

Promise & Potential Prayers

May you discover within yourself:
Wisdom to recognize your path,
Courage to navigate its course,
Strength to overcome the inevitable obstacles,
And will to joyfully persevere.

Have life abundantly.

May you wisely recognize the path plainly before you,
May you summon your courage to travel your path,
May you use your strength to love and to serve,
And may you choose to joyfully endure.

God's manifest blessings have been bestowed on your life.
Choose to animate and express them.

May you be blessed with:
Wisdom to recognize God,
Courage to welcome God,
Strength to embrace God,
And will to stay with God.

Both in life and in death we are one with God.

May you accept:
Wisdom to discern your purpose,
Courage to let go,
Strength to commit,
Faith to follow through.

The way is easy, the burden light.

And So It Begins...

We began with a simple premise; now we end with a profound revelation:

"If you can make the leap across the chasm of disbelief you succeed."

We have returned to where we began. The truth is, you possess the wisdom, courage, strength, and will to have life more abundantly. Live it!

To Be Happy
Spread happiness!

Pursue happiness,
The quarry eludes.

Multiply happiness,
And happiness will be found at every turn!

To have love
Give love!

Seek love,
The goal eludes.

Share love,
And love multiplies around you,
Securing you in its embrace!

Happiness and success are the blossoms of the blessings you share.

Scripture cautions us from believing any system of doctrine contains the entirety of truth, for in reality:

God's truth is infinite.

What Is
Came from How I was.

What Will Be
Comes from How I am.

When ego seeks power,
And arrogance dominates,
Seek not to submit,
Rather seek liberation,

Let go and all will be well.

Forgive trespassers,
By so doing you forgive yourself,
Then will you find your way home.

Afterword

It has been my pleasure to journey and explore together with you. You and I are, in truth, different aspects of one being.

As I began this undertaking, writing *Promise and Potential,* I had aspired and intended to capture words, ideas, and stories that entertain, inspire, and enlighten. You have hung in to the end, seen this reading through. I hope you have found something worthwhile. I hope you have discovered a glimmer of the promise and potential that is your life.

Whatever your impression of the expressions and ideas collected in these pages, I pray you read these last words with a growing sense of hope and optimism; a hope and optimism that springs from the realization you are closer to unlocking a mystery and truth you've possessed for a long time but didn't quite understand.

You continue — we continue on our journey together. The landscape continues to unfold, space and time continue to present challenges for our amusement and pleasure, our fulfillment. Keep moving forward; one little step is all it takes. Plunge in; the water is fine.

Have fun, keep the faith, embrace the truth:

You are goodness and truth,
You are whole, complete, loving and secure,
You are master of ego,
You are master of your experience.

My purpose working through the details of these ideas was to strengthen my own understanding and my own faith. By sharing I seek to join with you in building a bridge to a glorious homecoming. We, hand in hand, can find our way to where we belong.

Together we can sound the trumpet, light the fire, serve as beacons to call others home.

Attempting to capture dynamic ideas and affix them in text is clearly an exercise in the realm of the intellect. Though I've attempted to travel by way of emotion to spirit, the result (captured in these pages) being of intellect, is not truth. The best these words can do is focus energy to reach beyond intellect into the realm of spirit. You supply the energy. You transform the meaning from symbols on a page to experience. You are the catalyst for change.

For it is in the realm of spirit we are whole. Through the peace and joy of spirit we live fully, secure in the promise and potential of this life, my prayer for you…

All the best to you on your spiritual journey...

May the wind be at your back…

Until we meet again...

Recognize the promise, fulfill the potential…

Scott F. Paradis

. . . Then anyone who leaves behind him a written manual, and likewise anyone who receives it, in the belief that such writing will be clear and certain, must be exceedingly naïve.

- PLATO -

Acknowledgments

Promise and Potential is and always will be an evolving prayer made possible by the people that surround me, support me, and love me and those that are drawn into my awareness.

For my loving family — Lisa, my wife, and my two truly amazing children, Merideth and Mitchell, I am forever grateful.

To my sister, Renee, for her uncompromising support and encouragement I owe many thanks. Our journey of promise and potential continues.

To ancient writers and modern day prophets expressing truth through their words of insight and inspiration, I extend my thanks. I recommend the following for your consideration:

The Holy Bible

A Course in Miracles

And writings by: James Allen *(As A Man Thinketh);* Rhonda Byrne *(The Secret);* Deepak Chopra *(How to Know God; The Seven Spiritual Laws of Success* and many other titles); Russell H. Conwell *(Acres of Diamonds);* Wayne Dyer *(Wisdom of the*

Ages; The Power of Intention); David R. Hawkins *(The Eye of the I; Power vs. Force);* Guy Finley *(The Secret of Letting Go* and many other titles); Esther and Jerry Hicks *(Ask and It Is Given);* Gary Renard *(The Disappearance of the Universe; Your Immortal Reality);* Eckhart Tolle *(The Power of Now; A New Earth);* Neale Donald Walsh (*Conversations with God* series); and Gary Zukav *(The Seat of the Soul).*

This is only a small sample of those writers inspired to express wisdom. Though no words will capture the complete and awesome experience of Truth, know you can find it within.

Notes

1. Retelling and embellishment of a story that Guy Finley told during one of his spiritual principles teaching sessions. Further information about Guy Finley, his teachings, and his nonprofit foundation can be found at: *www.guyfinley.org.*
2. Adaptation of the "Creation Story" from the *Holy Bible* (the *Torah,* the *Pentateuch*), Book of Genesis, Chapters 1–3.

3a. From Primo Levi's memories of Auschwitz, chronicled in *Se questo e un uomo (If This Is a Man),* 1947; (Published in the U.S. as *Survival in Auschwitz,* 1958).

3b. From Primo Levi's analysis of the Auschwitz experience in his essay, *I sommersi e i salvati (The Drowned and the Saved),* 1986.

3c. From Primo Levi's *Se questo e un uomo (If This Is a Man),* 1947; (Published in the U.S. as *Survival in Auschwitz,* 1958).

3d. Recounted from an incident described in Elie Wiesel's memoir, *Night,* 1960.

3e. In addition to citations noted, the story of Father Maximillian Kolbe was compiled and quoted from biographies and historical accounts chronicled on the Internet at various sites:

http://www.cin.org/saints/maxkolbe.html
http://members.chello.nl/~l.de.bondt/KolbeEng.htm;
http://www.communityofhopeinc.org/
http://www.auschwitz.org.pl/
http://www.spectacle.org/
http://www.ushmm.org/

4. The story of Wilma Rudolph's life was taken from biographical accounts found at:
http://www.lkwdpl.org/wihohio/rudo-wil.htm
http://www.biggeststars.com/w/wilma-rudolph-biography.html
http://womenshistory.about.com/od/quotes/a/wilma_rudolph.htm and others.
5. Summaries from presidential biographies compiled from Internet sites:
http://www.whitehouse.gov/history/presidents
http://www.achievement.org
http://www.jimmycarterlibrary.org
http://www.reaganfoundation.org
http://bushlibrary.tamu.edu
http://www.clintonlibrary.gov/
http://www.biography.com/ and others.
6. Quoted and embellished from Russell H. Conwell's essay, *Acres of Diamonds* (public domain), delivered as a lecture thousands of times in the late nineteenth and early twentieth centuries. The original essay can be found at *http://www.temple.edu.*

Index

About the Author

Scott F. Paradis is a student of life and a seeker of ultimate truth. A native of New Hampshire, he has spent the last two decades traveling the world working national security issues, observing the remarkable similarities of people from diverse cultures, and pondering "weighty" questions: why are we here, and where are we headed?

Scott is married to a shining star, the former Lisa Newcombe, and has two wonderful children: a college-age daughter, Merideth, and a junior high school-age son, Mitchell.

Scott, a colonel in the U.S. Army, has had an eclectic career. Currently he serves at Department of the Army in strategic communications. Formerly he was a National Security Fellow at Harvard University's John F. Kennedy School of Government; he helped to establish the Multi-National Corps' counter improvised explosive device task force in Iraq; he was a military legislative assistant to a U.S. Senator, a deputy commander of an Army installation, a head of government relations for the Chief of the Army Reserve, and an aide-de-camp to the commanding general, Fifth U.S. Army. He also served in a variety of operational assignments, ranging from Operation Joint

Endeavor in the Balkans to assorted line and staff infantry officer positions.

His civilian work experience ranges from police officer, to real estate agent, to computer and life and health insurance sales, to fast food and manufacturing.

In addition to his nearly four years of formal military schooling, Scott holds a Bachelor of Arts degree in Sociology from the University of New Hampshire and a Master of Science degree in Administration from Central Michigan University.

Also from

CORNERSTONE ACHIEVEMENTS

&

Scott F. Paradis:

"Build Me A Son"
An original screenplay.
A journey of trial and triumph.

"Sounds of America"
A collection of Americana choral music.

And Coming Soon:

"The Money-Go-Round"
Realizing prosperity in this world.

Go to
www.cornerstone-achievements.com
for details.